East Anglia

Norman & June Buckley

Published by
Landmark Publishing Ltd
Waterloo House, 12 Compton, Ashbourne
Derbyshire, England DE6 1DA

Norman and June Buckley have more than 10 years experience in researching and writing guidebooks, both in Britain and continental Europe. They are keen walkers and many of their books focus on footpaths and other routes for walkers.

Norman is a keen environmentalist with qualifications in Environmental Management and Lake District Studies. June also holds qualifications in Tourism.

East Anglia has long been a favourite area and they have made many visits over the years. This comprehensive Visitor Guide follows Norman's *Guide to the Lake District* published in 1998, also in this series.

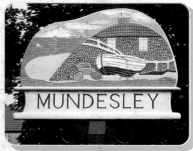

Village signs like these are popular in East Anglia
Opposite: *The Oliver Cromwell Museum in Ely*

LANDMARK VISITORS GUIDE

East Anglia

Norman & June Buckley

• Contents •

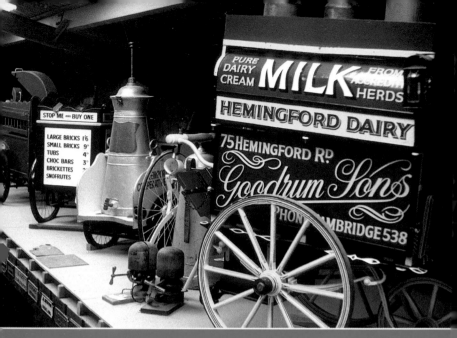

INTRODUCTION

Bulging out into the North Sea, flanked by a long coast line, the predominantly low-lying land which makes up East Anglia has always been a water dominated landscape. Rivers have never flowed swiftly and purposefully to the sea; they crawl along as if reluctant to give up their waters to the flat, marshy, estuaries, traditionally subject to flooding in prolonged or violent wet weather.

Since Roman times much energy, time and money has gone into elaborate drainage schemes, winning back thousands of rich alluvial acres from the water.

More dramatic is the sea's confrontation with the coast which is, for the most part, vulnerable with, at best, low, crumbling, cliffs. Here, the conflict takes two forms. Firstly there is the constant erosion, the creeping destruction caused by the ceaseless pounding at dunes, soft cliffs and modern sea defences. Land, villages and the occasional town have been lost to the sea over the centuries. The prime example is Dunwich,

Above: The Museum at Sutton Mill

progressively reduced by this elemental power from a considerable town, Bishopric and major port to the present day small village.

Secondly, the unfortunate combination of tides and winds can produce the 'North Sea Surge', with enormous tidal waves bursting through the defences. This happened in 1953 when much low-lying land in East Anglia was flooded, with great loss of life and property.

There is, however, a certain amount of give and take in the relationship between land and sea. Over a long period of time, silting has extended the North Norfolk coast into the Wash; former little ports such as Blakeney and Cley-next-the-Sea are now some distance inland. Similarly, the large town and port of Great Yarmouth has been built on a spit of land which has grown steadily since medieval times.

The final element in this watery landscape is the Norfolk (and Suffolk) Broads. Extensive digging of peat for fuel from Anglo-Saxon times to the early 14th century produced shallow but wide pits which, inevitably, flooded, producing the series of lakes and their connecting waterways which play a large part in today's East Anglian holiday economy.

Early History

Despite the threat posed by water, the area has long proved attractive to man. In pre-historic times access to this isolated area from the rest of England was difficult; the great watery barrier of the fens extended south almost as far as today's Cambridge and most of what is now Essex was covered in dense forest. The most attractive route was to use the chalk ridge to infiltrate into Breckland. Here, forest was relatively easy to clear and the light, sandy soil was easier to work than the heavy clays elsewhere in the area.

This became one of the country's most densely populated areas, with crop growing and cattle grazing to excess over the centuries producing a heath area vulnerable to sandstorms and over-populated by rabbits, a state of affairs not remedied until the 20th century, with the arrival of the Forestry Commission and mass planting of trees for commercial purposes. A very early industry, digging out and shaping flints, developed at Grimes Graves. In pre-historic times these were used as tools and weapons; in medieval times they became an important local building material.

Well before the arrival of the Romans, the population had become organised into tribes. Boudicca's rebellion against the Romans made the Iceni the best known. After the departure of the Romans, waves of Angle, Saxon and Jute invaders crossed the North Sea to arrive on the accessible shores, settling throughout

• Cycling •

East Anglia, being largely flat or rolling, and very rural, is wonderful cycling country. Most Rail services in the area allow travellers to take cycles. For specific advice ☎ 0345 484950. Cycle hire centres can be found in most parts of the region, and there are increasing numbers of cycling holidays on offer.

Keen cyclists should certainly have a copy of the Norfolk Cycling Map produced by Goldeneye Map Guides ☎ 01242 244889. This map is not cheap but it is showerproof and tear resistant. There are 10 rides on public highways plus 5 off-road routes, all clearly set out. The length varies from 21km (13 miles) to 59km (37 miles) and the rides are well spread throughout the county.

With the aid of a map it is easy to plan routes of any length linking the villages and attractions of the area, but suggested cycle rides are also included at the end of each chapter.

the area, developing agriculture, building churches, often with distinctive round towers, and burying special chieftains in great splendour, as at Sutton Hoo.

Despite the resistance led by Hereward the Wake, the Norman Conquest eventually prevailed in East Anglia. Churches were now built in Norman style, often modifying the earlier Anglo-Saxon buildings, and the whole area thrived, so much so that at the time of the Domesday Book the population density was among the highest in England.

Draining the Fens

The greatest landscape changes, however, occurred some centuries later with the draining of the fens. The Dutch engineer Cornelius Vermuyden and others enormously increased drainage of the still very extensive fen areas, straightening rivers, digging long, wide, drainage channels and pumping water from lower lying fields into these channels.

This achievement enabled agricultural pioneers such as Coke at Holkham and 'Turnip' Townshend of Raynham to transform much of East Anglia into probably the richest farming area in Britain, in the former case substituting wheat for the prevailing rye. There was also a side benefit in that navigation to inland ports such as Wisbech, Peterborough and Bedford was much improved.

Field and Village

The small fields, which existed long before the 19th century Parliamentary Enclosure Acts, have been expanded in the present century by the destruction of of old hedges to enable large and expensive agricultural machinery to function more efficiently.

The early enclosures also had a profound effect on the shape of many villages; in the classic English 'nuclear' village commonly owned fields are located around the outside of several closely grouped houses. In East Anglia, several hundred years earlier than elsewhere, common fields were divided and the land was grouped according to ownership, with a house built centrally within each holding of land, producing a spaced out, diffuse, village.

Wool Wealth

Before 18th century agricultural reform, sheep ruled the East Anglian economy for some centuries, generating great wealth for many merchants. 'Wool' towns and villages competed in displaying this wealth, usually by building great churches with rich flamboyant carvings.

Even more than in the churches, in the proliferation of vernacular architecture the builders of East Anglia have left a wealth of distinctive features which add immeasurably to the attraction of many towns and villages. Timber framing with plastered wattle and daub or brick nogging infill and, in some surviving cases, overhanging upper storeys, mixes happily with colour washed rendering, with or without pargetting.

Brick Nogging

Brick infilling between the uprights of timber-framed buildings. Sometimes, nogging was used to replace earlier wattle and daub, as the craft of daubing died out and bricks became cheaper and widely available.

Sometimes the brickwork is arranged in patterns: herringbone, chevron, horizontal or vertical.

Rural Isolation

For centuries Norwich was second only to London as England's largest city; however, the rural traditions of East Anglia, coupled with the absence of coal or iron ore deposits (hence no Industrial Revolution) discouraged the development of large cities, towns, or through trunkroads to other parts of the country.

Norwich, Cambridge and Ipswich are the biggest settlements, all now of comparatively modest size, an integral part of their environment rather than 'foreign' intrusions as a modern industrial city might be. They are all full of visitor interest and counted among England's great heritage places as, indeed, are

Top; Left: *By the River Thet at Thetford*
Right: *The Wells and Walsingham Railway at Walsingham* Below: *Beccles Quay*

Pargetting

Pargetry, parget-work or parge-work are all terms used to describe ornamental designs in plaster, either relief or incised. At first, designs were simple, incised into the wet plaster with a stick or group of sticks tied into a comb or fan shape.

The craft reached its height in the 17th century and flourished particularly in Suffolk and Essex – probably because the profusion of timber framed buildings in the region, for which this is a suitable decoration, and partly also because of the great wealth of these counties in the 16th and 17th centuries.

• Flint •

That awkward local material, flint, is at the very heart of East Anglian church building, great and small, and also of many less exalted buildings. Nowhere in the world has flint been used so extensively for building as in Norfolk and Suffolk. Look out for panels of dressed (knapped) flints which produce a patterned decorative effect known locally as 'flushwork', arranged with limestone or brick into decorative patterns in walls throughout the area.

Flint is found in the chalk band, a strange stone, it is one of the purest forms of silica and so hard as to be virtually indestructible, yet it can be easily fractured in any direction. This makes it an awkward building stone, but means it can be chipped and polished to a sharp edge for use as axe heads, farming implements and weapons.

Grimes Graves, near Thetford is one of the world's earliest industrial sites. Neolithic people mined flint here on a site covering 37 hectares, using only tools such as deer antler picks, polished flint axes and wooden shovels they dug pits up to 12 metres deep to extract the flint from where it lay buried beneath the chalk.

Flint work at Thetford Priory

• Nature Reserves •

East Anglia with its long, low coastline jutting out into the North Sea, its slow rivers, marshes and of course, The Broads, is a paradise for bird watchers. Nature reserves are widespread throughout the area and too numerous to mention in total; lists are widely available in the area. The most important reserves are included in the relevant chapters. The reserves listed below are operated by the Royal Society for the Protection of Birds. All have hides and trails; some have more comprehensive visitor facilities. Most are open to the public at all times

Ouse Washes
Welches Dam near Manea. *See also Chapter 1*
☎ 01354 680212.

Snettisham
On the shore of the Wash. Large numbers of wading birds, ducks and geese, particularly as the tide is rising. ☎ 01485 542689.

Titchwell Marsh
8km (5 miles) east of Hunstanton. Wetland reed beds and shallow lagoons. Ducks, geese and, in summer, the rare marsh harrier.
☎ 01485 210779.

Strumpshaw Fen
Near to Brundall, in the heart of the Norfolk Broads. Reedbeds and woodland. Swallowtail butterflies. Many birds, including bearded tits.
☎ 01603 715191.

Surlingham Church Marsh
On the opposite side of the River Yare to Strumshaw Fen, ten kilometres (6 miles) east of Norwich. Birds of reed and sedge fen, ditches and open water. ☎ 01508 538661.

Berney Marshes and Breydon Water
Accessed from the Asda car park near Great Yarmouth railway station. Grazing marshes and mudflats. ☎ 01493 700645.

Minsmere
A major visitor attraction, a flagship of the RSPB and a reserve of national importance. The large area of heath, woodland, marsh and lagoon, adjacent to the coast near Southwold, has nature trails, hides and a comprehensive visitor centre. *See also* Chapter 6.
☎ 01728 648281.

North Warren

1.5km (1 mile) north of Aldeburgh. Heathland, reedbeds and wet meadows. Wading birds including lapwings and redshanks breed here. White fronted geese, wigeons and shovelers in winter. ☎ 01728 688481.

Havergate Island

River Ore. Access only by the warden's boat from Orford Quay. Breeding place for avocets, sandwich and common terns. No ☎ number.

Stour Estuary

1.5km (1 mile) east of Wrabness. Wading birds, ducks and geese. In spring, nightingales and other song birds in adjacent woodland.
☎ 01255 886043.

Wolves Wood

3km (2 miles) east of Hadleigh. Coppiced ancient woodland. Wide variety of birds (including the nightingale in spring), plants and mammals.
☎ 01255 886043.

Fowlmere

11km (7 miles) south of Cambridge, between Fowlmere and Melbourne. Small wetland and chalk grassland reserve, with reedbeds and disused watercress beds.
☎ 01763 261259.

many of the smaller towns and villages.

In recent years, encouraged and promoted by an active Tourist Board, visitor attractions have increased in number, for example more farms and vineyards have opened their premises to the public, walking and cycle trails have been created, whilst Tourist Information Centres have increased their assistance to the public, including the provision of accommodation booking services in most cases.

It all adds up to an area of distinctive overall character yet, within that character, a wide diversity of landscape, of buildings and of monuments, with activities available to suit virtually any visitor.

Inevitably, this distinctive area has either bred or attracted its fair share of legendary figures, from Boudicca to Benjamin Britten. Others we shall meet in this book include Oliver Cromwell, Horatio (Lord) Nelson, John Constable and Thomas Gainsborough.

Wildlife

Because of the lack of polluting industry and the wide open spaces, wildlife has always been abundant, the Fens, the Broads and the coast being particularly famous for waterfowl. This has been recognised by the creation of numerous reserves, some of national and even international importance.

1 FENLAND

The Fenland landscape – huge, wide open spaces, generally as flat as a pancake and threaded with drainage channels great and small – is often thought, wrongly, to characterise East Anglia as a whole.

What is generally regarded as 'Fenland' extends well into Lincolnshire in the north, outside the scope of this book about East Anglia, and to the fringe of Cambridge in the south, a total of more than 80km (50 miles). From Peterborough in the west to Lakenheath and Mildenhall in the east the width averages about 50km (30 miles). Some of the western fringe is in Huntingdonshire and North-amptonshire, again outside the scope of this book.

Much of this area is below sea level and the thriving agriculture on its rich soil depends on the maintenance of complex drainage systems.

Towns, largely built on the pre-drainage era 'islands', are few and far between and even the villages are well spaced. Many visitors might consider this to be a boring countryside but, for

Above: North Brink at Wisbech

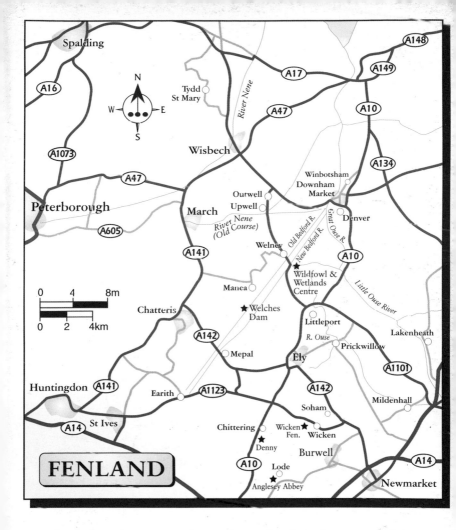

those who value peace and tranquillity, the vast uninterrupted skies, and the length and breadth of view from a modest elevation such as a bridge are something very special indeed.

As would be expected in an area so well endowed with water and comparatively under-populated, the fen area is rich in wildlife, with a dominance of waterfowl. The many nature reserves make it easy to enjoy the sight of great flocks of a variety of birds, some being resident whilst others are summer or winter visitors.

Intensive cultivation of the dark rich soil includes large areas of cereals (wheat and barley) and root crops (sugar beet, potatoes and carrots). To the north, around Wisbech, are apple orchards and other fruit growing (strawberries, raspberries and blackberries). Further north, around Spalding are flowers, including the famous bulb fields.

Overall, there are more than 1000 farms, employing over 4000 people. The trend is towards fewer and larger farm units and, over the last 50 years there has been much criticism of the progressive removal of hedgerows, with the consequent creation of 'prairies' and the loss of topsoil in dry, windy, weather. The livestock grazing which was formerly dominant on the wet fen land has diminished accordingly.

So, what does this highly distinctive area offer today's visitor?

Apart from the interest of the historic towns, there is a surprising array of attractions, many of them based on Fenland history and tradition and many on the abundant wildlife and its protection. Pleasure boating on the many linked waterways is a special attraction of the area.

Wisbech and Downham Market

Visitors travelling from the North and Midlands will approach East Anglia through Fenland and will already have a taste of the distinctive countryside before reaching Wisbech, a medieval port and considerable market town, centre of a thriving agricultural region.

Wisbech's great days as a port were when the coastline of The Wash was much further south than at present. Early drainage efforts, coupled with natural silting, have left the town 19km (12 miles) inland. However the port, reached via the artificial channel of the River Nene, is still active for vessels of up to 1500 tons, trading principally with the Low Countries.

The town has a great deal of elegant Georgian architecture, seen at its best in the long terraces of **North Brink** and **South Brink**, on either side of the river, and in The Crescent and adjacent terraces. The old is well complemented by the newer shopping centre close to the Market Place. Markets are held each Thursday and Saturday.

Probably the best of the many 18th century houses is **Peckover House (1722)** with good gardens, now owned by the National Trust. The house was bought at the end of the 18th century by Jonathan Peckover, a member of a Quaker banking family. Although a little plain outside, the interior is elegant, with fine panelling and Georgian fireplaces.

The church of **St Peter** and **St Paul** has a long and varied architectural history, including portions dating from the 12th century. The interior is light with a sense of space. The 16th century tower has a unique peal of ten bells.

After the Brinks, the best Georgian buildings are seen in the area of the former castle, where crescents of houses follow the line of the old moat, demonstrating the 18th century prosperity of the town. There was a Norman castle here, built to subdue the wild fenmen, replaced in turn by a Bishop's palace in 1478, a mansion in the 17th century and then the present Regency villa in 1816. The gate piers are all that remain of the mansion.

The **Wisbech and Fenland Museum** in Museum Square was founded in 1835. The wide ranging collection includes memorabilia of local families such as the Peckovers, together with geology, zoology, topography and history exhibits. There is a gallery for temporary exhibitions. The striking monument close to the Town Bridge is to Thomas Clarkson, born in Wisbech, who devoted much of his life to the campaign against slavery. The design is by Gilbert Scott.

At 1, South Brink Place, the **Octavia Hill Birthplace Museum** honours the woman who was not only one of the three founders of the National Trust, but who also spent the greater part of her life working to improve the housing conditions of the poorest sections of society, initiating many improvement and rebuilding schemes, particularly in London. The 'Florence Nightingale of Victorian Housing', she created housing management as a profession.

The **Angles Theatre** is a multi-purpose arts centre housed in a Georgian building, with a long theatrical tradition.

Some distance along North Brink is an old brewery, in use for two hundred years. The Elgood family have produced fine ales here since 1878 and have opened the premises and the four acres of splendid garden to the public, with guided tours on some days.

The **Tourist Information Centre** is centrally situated, close to the Town Bridge and the Clarkson Monument. Included is an exhibition of historic photographs of the locality by the late Lilian Ream.

Places close to Wisbech

Butterfly and Falconry Park at Long Sutton is one of the country's largest indoor butterfly gardens, a 'tropical world' of plants, flowers, ponds and butterflies. Falconry displays are given twice daily. A picnic area, tearoom and gift shop are included.

The **African Violet Centre** at Terrington St Clement is a unique nursery, specialising in this well-loved plant. It has a tearoom and gift shop.

At the **Fenland and West Norfolk Aviation Museum** at Bamber's Garden Centre, Old

• Boating •

The Fens provide favourite cruising waters for those who value peace and tranquillity, with level landscapes and a minimum of locks. The extensive system is contained within an area of about 60km (36 miles) by 50km (30 miles). The waterways connect towns and cities such as Cambridge, Peterborough, Ely, March and Ramsey and many villages.

Principal navigations are the River Great Ouse and its tributaries, the River Nene-Ouse Navigation link, with tributaries, and the Rivers Cam, Lark and Wissey.

Also available for navigation, but of less visitor interest, is the New Bedford River, tidal and cut straight from near Earith to Denver Sluice near to Downham Market. Hire craft are not permitted along this waterway. North of Denver Sluice the River Great Ouse is tidal and is potentially dangerous for pleasure craft.

Beyond the fens there are links through Peterborough and Northampton to the Grand Union Canal and the main inland waterway system and also via Earith to Huntingdon and Bedford.

Marinas and organised moorings are available at 20 sites throughout the area included in this book, but not all have the full range of facilities.

Boat hire ranges from small day boats for a few hours use to motor cruisers and narrow boats for holiday use:

Fox Boats
March, Traditional narrow boats. ☎ 01354 652770.

Daymond Services
Denver Sluice, Downham Market, Day boats and holiday cruisers. ☎ 01366 384404.

The Boat Haven
Littleport near Ely, Day boats. ☎ 01353 863763.

Bridge Boat Yard
Ely, Holiday cruisers for short breaks and weekly hire. ☎ 01353 663726.

Mepal Outdoor and Activity Centre
Mepal, Chatteris, Sailing, canoeing, windsurfing hire. Courses on inland lake. ☎ 01354 692251.

Sailing facilities are available at **Denver Sailing Club**, Denver Sluice, near Downham Market.

Navigation Authorities

River Nene, River Great Ouse and tributaries
Environment Agency, Orton Goldhay, Peterborough, Cambs. ☎ 01733 371811.

Nene-Ouse Navigation Link
Middle Level Commissioners, Dartford Road, March, Cambs. ☎ 01354 653232.

Boats moored on the river at March

Lynn Road, Wisbech there is a display of aviation artifacts and memorabilia. There are three planes, a jumbo jet cockpit simulator and a souvenir shop.

Marshland Smeeth and Fen Museum is at Tilney Fen End, just off the A47 at Terrington St John. There is a display of diesel engines and pumps in working order.

Outwell and Upwell are pleasant linear waterside villages along the old course of the River Nene, on the way to the modest market town, **Downham Market**, built on rising ground on the eastern fringe of the fens. Notable in the Market Place is a black and white monument with clock, presented to the town in 1878.

Across the river on the west of the town, a right turn from the A1122 in a short distance, followed by another right turn into a minor trackway, and then yet another right turn in about half a kilometre (one third of a mile) leads to the remarkable **Collector's World of Eric St John Foti** at Hermitage Hall and Bridge Farm. First is a building with farming and other varied bygones, a collection of Armstrong Siddeley cars.

Across the yard is the truly fantastic part of this attraction, visited only by guided tour, with very restricted opening hours. Starting in the Pilgrims' Hall, the visitor proceeds through the chapel, re-dedicated for worship in recent years, and then past a permanent Nativity scene and a claimed splinter of the true cross. Next comes the Nelson room, library, the Bell Courtyard and the refectory, where hot tots of Norfolk punch are served. This drink was reintroduced by Foti after his discovery of a medieval recipe.

Finally comes a wonderfully detailed re-creation of the English town of about 100 years ago with extensive exhibits such as old shops, complete with authentic sounds. There is a special feature on the romantic novelist Barbara Cartland. Most of the collection is housed in former farm buildings, the plain exteriors giving little clue to the internal interest and complexity.

To the south of Downham Market, is **Denver Sluice**, a key feature in Fenland drainage schemes, with engineering work by the great John Rennie. The sluice separates the South level river system from the tidal Great Ouse and the sea. There are river moorings for pleasure craft, an inn and a car park and picnic area, with public conveniences. Close to the sluice, Denver tower windmill is open to visitors.

South of Denver, accessed by a narrow fenland road, is the important **reserve at Welney** operated by the Wildfowl and Wetlands Trust. A modest visitor centre, with tearoom, is located on the edge of The Washes, with access to a considerable area of land and extensive well-spaced observation hides.

Peckover House and Garden

(National Trust), North Brink. Tearoom with light lunches. Open from late March to the end of October, Saturdays, Sundays and Bank Holiday Mondays, 12.30 to 17.30. Garden only, Mondays, Tuesdays and Thursdays, same hours. Cafe.
☎ 01945 583463.

Wisbech and Fenland Museum

Museum Square. Open Tuesdays to Saturdays, 10.00 to 17.00 April to September. (October to March from 10.00 to 16.00).
☎ 01945 583817.

Octavia Hill Birthplace Museum

1, South Brink Place. Open from the beginning of March to the end of October, Wednesdays, Saturdays and Sundays, 14.00 to 17.30.
☎ 01945 476358.

Elgood's Brewery and Garden

North Brink. Visitor centre, museum, shop and teas. Garden open from mid-April to late September, Wednesdays, Thursdays, Fridays, Saturdays, Sundays and Bank Holidays, 13.30 to 17.30. Brewery tours: Wednesdays, Thursdays and Fridays, 14.30.
☎ 01945 583160.

Butterfly and Falconry Park

Long Sutton. Shop, restaurant and tearoom. Open late March to end of October, daily from 10.00 to 18.00 (September and October from 10.00 to 17.00).
☎ 0106 363833.

African Violet Centre

Terrington St Clement. Gift shop and tearoom. Open daily from 10.00 to 17.00 (not Christmas or New Year).
☎ 01553 828374.

Fenland and West Norfolk Aviation Museum

Bamber's Garden Centre, Old Lynn Road. Open weekends and Bank Holidays, April to September, 9.30 to 17.00 (March and October 10.00 to 16.30). Tearoom at garden centre.
☎ (secretary) 01945 584440.

21

Marshland Smeeth and Fen Museum

Tilney Fen End, Terrington St John. Open selected days only, usually the second Sunday of the month from May to October.

Collector's World of Eric St John Foti

Hermitage Hall, off the A1122 close to Downham Market. Gift shop and tearoom. Open Easter until the last Sunday before Christmas, Sundays, Fridays and Bank Holidays, 13.00 to 17.00. ☎ 01366 383185.

Wildfowl and Wetlands Trust

Welney. Gift/book shop and tearoom. Open daily from 10.00 to 17.00. (except Christmas Day).
☎ 01353 860711.

Denver Mill

Open from Easter to the end of September, Wednesdays, Saturdays, Sundays and Bank Holidays, 14.00 to 16.00.
☎ 01366 383374.

Above: The Welney Wildlife and Wetlands Trust
Right: Denver Mill

Ely Cathedral

Ely

Despite its compact size, Ely is one of the focal points of the fens, standing on the largest of the old 'islands', no less than 21m (68 feet) high. Ely's crowning glory is the great cathedral, visible for miles in all directions, as it soars above the town. The religious origins of this site go back to the 7th century when St Etheldreda founded an abbey here.

From Ely, Hereward the Wake and his followers provided the last Anglo-Saxon resistance to the Norman invasion for several years, harrying the invaders then retreating into the watery fastness by tortuous routes. He was betrayed in 1071, when he became lost to history. The marshes which sheltered Hereward were largely drained in the 17th century.

Around the cathedral is a range of former monastic buildings; outstanding are the 14th century **Porta**, now part of the King's School, the **Great Hall**, now the Bishop's residence and the 15th century **Bishop's Palace**, now used as a Sue Ryder home.

Modern Ely has a modest shopping centre, with a street market each Thursday; there is also a sports centre.

Ely Museum is housed in a former gaol, with the exercise yard serving as the forecourt. Local history of the Isle of Ely and the cathedral city is featured.

Oliver Cromwell House in St Mary's Street is best approached across Palace Green, in front of the cathedral. Oliver Cromwell and his family lived here from 1636-47. Several rooms of this most interesting visitor attraction are furnished in period and there are displays concerning the Civil War, with an array of 17th century clothing for visitors to try. Audio commentary is available. There is also an audio-visual presentation on fenland drainage, a gift shop and the Ely Tourist Information Centre. The house itself is claimed to have early 13th century origins.

On the eastern edge of the city there is a riverside area, with extensive boat moorings and other facilities, a focal point of the Fenland waterway system. An old maltings building has been converted to an arts centre with cafe and a former warehouse is now a large antiques centre. With the adjacent willow-fringed waterway, this is a most attractive part of the city.

Ely Cathedral

The present cathedral was begun in the 11th century and it has dominated the small city ever since. In 1342 the original central tower collapsed and was replaced by the present splendidly unique octagonal tower. Most of the original Norman work is now found in the west front, the nave and the transepts. The long, high, nave has a delicately painted ceiling; there is a fine altarpiece and lovely stone carving in and adjacent to the chapels at the east end of the building. The modern statue of Jesus with Mary Magdalene is by David Wynne. The cathedral includes a museum of stained glass, a gift shop and varied catering.

The railway station has services on the line running from Norwich to Peterborough, with connections north and south.on the East Coast Main line, also a line to Cambridge, with services to London.

Places Close to Ely

Prickwillow Drainage Engine Museum lies about 6km (4 miles) to the north-east. The museum has a well presented collection of the powerful pumping engines which succeeded the previous wind and steam-powered pumps. Occasionally, on special days, engines are run for the benefit of visitors.

A few kilometres south of Ely is **Wicken** village and the important **National Nature Reserve of Wicken Fen**. With adjacent Fen Cottage, the reserve and its visitor centre are operated by the National Trust. The reserve is situated at Lode Lane, a close community of Fen people dating from the 17th century onwards. During the 18th and 19th centuries the cutting of turf, sedge and reeds provided local employment and created wealth.

Fen Cottage is a restoration of no. 5, Lode Lane, bought by the Trust in 1974 and renovated from 1988. The fen itself is a nutrient-rich low-lying wetland with a variety of walks into its heart, along lush green paths, a surviving remnant of the former 'Great Fen of East Anglia'. The nearby

Wicken windpump was the last working wooden windpump in East Anglia. It was moved from a nearby fen and rebuilt at Wicken in 1956.

A little way to the east, at the south end of Soham, is **Downfield Mill**. Further south is **Burwell Museum**, a village museum housed in a re-erected timber-framed barn, with smithy and wheelwright's workshop, wagons, carts, tractors and period displays.

Anglesey Abbey, owned by the National Trust, is situated at Lode, off the Burwell to Cambridge road. The house was built in 1600, on the site of an Augustinian Priory. The garden has been created since the 1930s, a wonderful combination of avenues with wide grassy walks lined by trees and with historic statuary. There is also a working watermill. The house furnishings are sumptuous, with many fine paintings. There is also a plant centre, shop and restaurant.

Denny Abbey, about 10km (6 miles) north of Cambridge on the Ely road, is a combination of the abbey remains with a farming and village life museum, administered by English Heritage. The Abbey has had a varied life. After Benedictine monks came Knights Templar and, following abolition of the Knights, the buildings were taken over and extended in 1327 by the Countess of Pembroke for occupation by Poor Clare nuns. In more recent centuries there

• Oliver Cromwell •

Oliver Cromwell was one of the handful of outstanding characters who have shaped the destiny of the nation. As the ultimate leader of the Parliamentary forces in the Civil War, the creator of the 'New Model Army' and the man who deposed and then had the legitimate sovereign, King Charles I, executed, Cromwell certainly made his mark on our history. From 1653 until his death in 1658, the title 'Lord Protector' formalised his position as effectively the ruler of the land.

Cromwell was very much a man of East Anglia, born on 25th April, 1599 at Huntingdon, just a few miles to the west of Cambridge and Ely. After education at the local grammar school, he spent a year at Sidney Sheldon College, Cambridge before returning to the family on the death of his father in 1617.

Further studies at the Inns of Court in London were followed by marriage to Elizabeth Bourchier in 1620 and the leasing of a farm at St. Ives, again a short distance to the west of Cambridge. A period of happy family life followed, with children, eight in all, arriving at comparatively short intervals.

THE HOME OF OLIVER CROMWELL AND HIS FAMILY. CROMWELL ROSE TO POWER DURING THE ENGLISH CIVIL WARS, TO BECOME "LORD PROTECTOR OF THE COMMONWEALTH" DURING ENGLAND'S BRIEF PERIOD AS A REPUBLIC IN THE MID 17TH CENTURY. THE CROMWELL FAMILY LIVED IN ELY FOR SOME TEN YEARS FROM 1636 TO 1646.

In 1636 he inherited a substantial estate, including the house in Ely now known as Cromwell House, from his maternal uncle. This inheritance also brought him a job as local tax collector - the tithes of two Ely parishes - to be paid over to the Dean and Chapter of the cathedral, with the responsibility of paying the church chaplains and for some building maintenance.

The commemorative plaque to Oliver Cromwell at Ely

Any excess of collection was retained by Cromwell as his fee, enhancing his local status as a man of property. He became spokesman for the local fen people in their opposition to the major drainage schemes which they believed would damage their traditional, largely water-based, livelihood. This activity earned him the derisory title of 'Lord of the Fens' from political opponents.

Cromwell loved the countryside, enjoying the pursuits appropriate to his status such as horse riding, hunting and hawking. He and his family had moved into 'Cromwell House' in 1636, staying until 1647, by which time the Civil War had been won, and the King would lose his head a year later.

Oliver was born into a Puritan household and his beliefs were nurtured and strengthened throughout his education, strongly conditioning his inflexible attitude towards worship, music and ornamentation inside churches and to the government of the country. Cromwell House in Ely is open to the public.

have been further changes to the buildings; noteworthy is the large stone refectory.

The linked farmland and village life museum has old machinery, dairy equipment, blacksmith's workshop and exhibits on Cambridgeshire landscapes and crop varieties. There is a refreshment room.

Chatteris is an unassuming small fenland town. Close by is the **Ouse Washes Nature Reserve** and wildlife visitor centre at Welches Dam, approached via Manea.

Stonea Camp, off the B1093 south-east of March, signposted 'Stitches Farm', enjoys the distinction of being the lowest-lying Iron Age hill fort in Britain, with defensive embankments constructed on a low 'island'. The fort was taken by the Romans and subsequently levelled. It was restored following archaeological excavations in 1991. It is also a valuable wildlife refuge, with barn owls. Wild flower seeds have been sown and a pond has been cleared of farm rubbish.

Another fenland town on a raised 'island', grew and prospered as a trading and religious centre and minor port. March is now a market town (Wednesday and Saturday) catering for a considerable surrounding area. Broad Street is well named as part of the main thoroughfare, lined with shops and with the ornate 'fountain' erected in 1911 to commemorate the coronation of King George V.

The River Nene, easily overlooked, winds through the town, part of the Fenland waterway system, with moorings and other boat user facilities conveniently situated in the town centre and a marina on the outskirts. The river is well seen from the riverside gardens off the main street.

St Wendreda's Church at Town End, on the southern fringe of March, is medieval, with a magnificent double hammer beam roof, 120 carved angels and other interesting features.

The railway station, once an important junction with large marshalling yards, now has services on the Norwich to Ely and Peterborough line

March Museum occupies a former school building in High Street, with a wide-ranging collection of domestic, agricultural and other local artifacts. There are displays of life at the turn of the century.

North of March is **Stags Holt Farm Park**, with Suffolk Punch horses, other animals and farming bygones housed in Victorian farm buildings.

Places to Visit
In & Around Ely & March

Ely Museum

The Old Goal, Market Street. Open all year, Tuesday to Sunday and Bank Holiday Mondays, 10.30 to 16.30. ☎ 01353 666655.

Oliver Cromwell House

29, St Mary's Street, Ely. Open January to March and October to December, Monday to Saturday, 10.00 to 17.15. April to September, daily, 10.00 to 18.00. Closed Christmas Day, Boxing Day and New Year's Day. ☎ 01353 662062.

Prickwillow Drainage Engine Museum

Main Street, Prickwillow. Open from January to March, Saturday, Sunday and Bank Holiday Mondays, 11.00 to 16.00. April to October, Monday to Friday, 10.00 to 17.00; Saturday and Sunday, 11.00 to 16.00. November and December, Saturday and Sunday, 11.00 to 16.00. Light refreshments. ☎ 01353 688360.

Wicken Fen Nature Reserve

(National Trust), off the A1123. Visitor centre open all year, daily, 09.00 to 17.00. Fen Cottage open Sunday afternoons in season. ☎ 01353 720274.

Downfield Windmill

Fordham Road, Soham. Open all year, Sunday and Bank Holiday Mondays, 11.00 to 17.00. Closed Christmas week. ☎ 01353 720333.

Burwell Museum

Mill Close, Burwell. Open from mid-April to late September, Thursday Sunday and Bank Holiday Mondays, 14.00 to 17.00. ☎ Tourist Information Centre Ely, Newmarket or Cambridge.

Anglesey Abbey

(National Trust), at Lode off the B1102 Burwell to Cambridge road. House open from late March to mid-October, Wednesday to Sunday and Bank Holiday Mondays, 13.00 to 17.00. Garden more frequently open – consult N.T. Handbook or ☎ 01223 811200.

Denny Abbey and Farmland Museum

Ely Road, Chittering. (English Heritage). Cafe. Open from late March to the end of October, daily, 12.00 to 17.00. ☎ 01223 860480.

Welches Dam

Near Manea. Ouse Washes Nature Reserve. One hide accessible to the disabled. Visitor Centre open daily, 09.00 to 17.00. ☎ 01354 680212.

March and District Museum

High Street, March. Open all year, Wednesday, 10.00 to 12.00; Saturday, 10.00 to 12.00 and 14.00 to 16.00. Closed from before Christmas to the early New Year. ☎ 01354 655300.

Stags Holt Farm Park

Signposted from the B1101 March to Coldham road, 5km (3 miles) north-east of March. Tearoom and picnic area. Children's play area. Caravan park. Open daily during early bank holidays, more widely during May to August, 1030 to 1700. ☎ 01354 652406.

With its great fields of productive agricultural land, today's Fenland landscape is highly artificial. For thousands of years after the final departure of the last ice age, the Wash coastline lay several miles to the south of its present position, with an inland waterscape of wilderness marshes surrounding the relatively few small islands, inhabited since prehistoric times. Man's determination to wrest more usable agricultural land from this watery waste continued from Bronze Age through Roman, Anglo-Saxon and Medieval times up to the present day, forming the backbone of Fenland history.

The natural silting processes around the rivers played their part in altering the coastline of the Wash. Subsequent drainage, largely by the construction of raised banks, helped in a partial drying out process. Between the 11th and the 13th centuries, the land-owning monasteries played a major part in the construction of these banks.

After several centuries of relative inactivity, the favourable economic circumstances of the 17th century brought major attempts at further drainage, led by the Earl of Bedford. Experienced engineers were brought from the Low Countries, most notably Cornelius Vermuyden, to tackle the remaining undrained silt fens in the north and the peat fens of the south.

Despite hostility from many locals who believed their traditional fishing and wildfowling way of life was threatened, work pressed on and the great constructions of the Old and New Bedford Rivers, stretching from Earith to Denver, with many ancillary works, were completed.

These were effective but, as the land dried out, it began to shrink until the rivers became higher than the fields they were supposed to drain. The answer provided by the Dutch engineers was, of course, windpumps, hundreds of windpumps, successful only when the wind blew. From the time of the Industrial Revolution these pumps were progressively replaced by steam driven pumps then, in turn, diesel engines and today's electric motors.

Today the land is kept usable by a sophisticated network of embanked rivers, natural and artificial, high above the fields, and the network of channels from which water is raised to the rivers by powerful electrically driven pumps. Side benefits include recreations such as boating and angling, and the rich and diverse wildlife.

Many relics of this fascinating history have been preserved; some can be seen at Prickwillow, Stretham and the Marshland Smeeth and Fen engine museums. There is an excellent short video film to be seen at the Oliver Cromwell museum in Ely. Additionally, several of the old windpumps have been restored.

Above: A recreation of abbey life at Denny Abbey
Right: The Ship Inn, March
Below: The Farm Museum at Denny Abbey

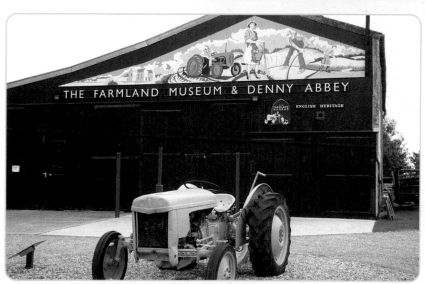

Walks: Fenland

Whilst few people would claim that Fenland is prime walking country scenically, there is, nevertheless, a good range of footpaths. The rich diversity of the wildlife, with abundant nature reserves, waterside settlements and relics such as windpumps all under skies which can be truly dramatic, compensate for the flatness of the landscape.

Details of these and other possible walks can be obtained from Tourist Information Centres.

1 The Peter Scott Walk

Named after the late and great ornithologist who lived for several years in the 1930s in the east lighthouse by the mouth of the River Nene. The walk has possible starting places at car parks at West Lynn, Ongar Hill and Sutton Bridge, with the route traversing the fairly recently constructed sea bank, through the remote Wash salt marshes. Since the time of Sir Peter Scott's residence, a further mile of land has been reclaimed.

The full walk is just over 16km (10 miles); the intermediate starting points give walks of 11km (7 miles) and 6.5km (4 miles).

2 Wimbotsham Parish Walk

Typical of the 31 short, village-based walks included in a 'Norfolk Walks' pack published by Norfolk County Council, Planning and Transportation Department, in association with the Country-side Commission. Available at Tourist Information Centres.

The Wimbotsham walk is a maximum of 5km (3 miles) in length, with shorter options. It is waymarked throughout. Start at the village centre, head north to join Longchurch Lane, turning left along the lane. Continue past Gravelpit Plantation and Whinclose Covert. Turn left at the far end of the covert, then left again at the south west corner to take the obvious route back into Winbotsham. Wimbotsham is 3km (2 miles) north of Downham Market, along the B1507.

↑3 The Washes

There are linear paths along either side of the Washes area, between the Old and New Bedford Rivers. There are only two points at which this great length of land can be crossed. One crossing is about 6km (4 miles) south-west of Downham Market. Using this crossing gives a circular walk of about 8km (5 miles) to and from Salters Lode. Wildlife is very much the focus of this walk.

↑4 Wicken Fen

A 4km (2 mile) nature trail and a 1km (0.75 mile) walk on a boarded way are available at this visitor attraction.

↑5 Fen Rivers Way

One of several designated routes, running for almost 28km (17 miles) along the sides of the River Great Ouse and the River Cam, between Ely and Cambridge.

↑6 Nene Way

Another designated riverside route, starting at the 'Dog in a Doublet' pub near Whittlesey, passing through Wisbech to reach the end at Sutton Bridge, 40km (25 miles) distant.

↑7 Hereward Way

This long distance (176km / 110 mile) route passes through Fenland, including Peterborough, March and Ely, before heading out of the fens towards Thetford.

For those who hate riding bicycles uphill the Fens are cycling country par excellence. The sparse population means great expanses of open countryside and, with a few exceptions, quiet roads. Having said that, strong headwinds are not uncommon and many Fenland roads are sufficiently narrow for passing cars to create something of a hazard. Nevertheless, cycling is a wonderful way to tour in the Fens, the leisurely progress permitting full appreciation of the landscape, with periodic highlights of friendly towns and villages, no parking problems and choices of welcoming inns and tearooms.

A free leaflet with map **A Guide to Cycling in the Fens**, widely available from Tourist Information Centres, suggests fifteen circular itineraries ranging from 21km (13 miles) to 62km (38.5 miles). For longer rides, some of these routes lend themselves well to combination. The leaflet also has useful information on cycle sales and repairs, cycle hire and cycling clubs. The suggestions include:

1 Wisbech and Tydford St Giles

A quiet route exploring the silt fens to the north-west of Wisbech. Impressive churches and houses. Particularly attractive countryside at orchard blossom time. 28km (17.5 miles).

2 March and Stonea

A short ride to the Stonea iron age settlement, returning to March by a different route. 21km (13 miles).

3 Ely and Soham

Mostly on quiet country roads, this ride explores the fens to the south and east of Ely. The pumping engine museum at Prickwillow and the working windmill at Soham are added attractions along the way. 41km (25.5 miles).

↑1 North Norfolk Coast

From a Fenland base, drive along the north Norfolk coast, via King's Lynn. This route includes the opportunity to visit Sandringham, Hunstanton, Brancaster and many other places described in detail in Chapter 2.

↑2 Cambridge, Newmarket, Bury St Edmunds, Thetford and its Forest

These places can be linked in a very rewarding circuit. Better still, allow a full day for a Cambridge visit and combine the other places. Details can be found in Chapters 9, 7 and 5 respectively.

The River Cam, Cambridge

↑3 The 'Dorothy L. Sayers Tour of the Fens'

For those interested in the life and work of the great novelist and playright, creator of Lord Peter Wimsey. Stretching from Earith to Kings Lynn see leaflet obtainable from appropriate Tourist Information Centres such as Ely (☎ 01353 662062) Further information from The Dorothy L. Sayers Society (☎ 01273 833444).

Hotels

Ely

The Lamb Hotel, old coaching inn, ☎ 01353 663574 Fax 662023

Wisbech

The White Lion Hotel, South Brink ☎ 01945 463060 Fax 463069

March

The Old Griffin Hotel ☎ 01354 652517

Guest Houses and B&B

Upwell near Wisbech

The Olde Mill ☎ and Fax 01945 772614

Downham Market

The Dial House ☎ 01366 388358 Fax 382238

Nr Wisbech

Stratton Farm, Walton Highway ☎ 01945 880162

Nr Ely

Hill House Farm, Coveney ☎ 01353 778369

Nr Downham Market

Crosskeys Riverside Hotel, Hilgay ☎ 01366 387777

Downham Market

The Dial House, Railway Road ☎ 01366 388358 Fax 382238

Wisbech

Bramley Cottage, Sutton Road ☎ 01945 463132

Self-catering

Nr Wisbech

Three cottages at Guyhirn, 5 miles from Wisbech Contact Mrs Eliot ☎ 01945 450425

Wisbech

Bank Cottage Holiday Cottages ☎ 01945 450425

Caravan and Camping Sites

Peterborough

Ferry Meadows Caravan Club Site ☎ 01733 233526

Nr March

Floods Ferry Caravan Park 3 miles from March ☎ 01354 677302

Eating Out

Ely

The Cathedral Refectory Dominiques, St Mary's Street ☎ 01353 665011

Nr Downham Market

The Hare Arms, Stow Bardolph ☎ 01366 382229

This very rural area has a predominance of small scale local arts and crafts exhibitions. Some of the well-established events are given here.

East of England Show
The Showground
Peterborough. Late July.
☎ 01733 234451

Littleport Show
Usually including medieval jousting. Late July.

Ely Horticultural Show
Late August.
☎ 01353 860229

Fenland Country Fair
Quy Park, Stow cum Quy,
Cambs. Late August.
☎ 01638 742845

Flower Festival
Wisbech. Early September.
☎ 01945 582476

Wildlife Day
Wicken Fen. Early
September.
☎ 01353 720274

Steam Engine Rally
Haddenham, near Ely.
Mid-September.
☎ 01487 841893

Chatteris Festival
Late June.
☎ 01354 692769

Wisbech Rose Fair
Early July.
☎ Tourist Information Centre
01945 583263

**Wisbech Horticultural
Open Day**
Mid-May.
☎ 01945 581024

**Spalding Flower
Parade and Carnival**
Early May.
☎ 01775 725468

Wisbech Weekend
Packed with special events.
Mid-May and mid-
September.
☎ 01945 583263

Ely Folk Festival
Mid-July.
☎ 01353 741032

2 KINGS LYNN & NORTH-WEST NORFOLK

The countryside fringing the Fenlands soon becomes more rolling, with a long, low, chalky ridge running roughly north to south and good quality farmland prevailing. The large and important town of Kings Lynn at the western end is contrasted by the attractions of the more easterly coastal towns and villages such as Hunstanton, Wells-next-the-Sea and Brancaster. Historic and interesting towns include Little Walsingham, Fakenham and East Dereham, and there are numerous villages, stately homes and other attractions.

The coast is among the finest in East Anglia; great swathes of sand, former tiny ports and literally mile upon mile of nature reserves.

Kings Lynn

A very old port and a considerable town, **Kings Lynn** still has many signs of its former wealth

Above: The Bull Inn, Little Walsingham

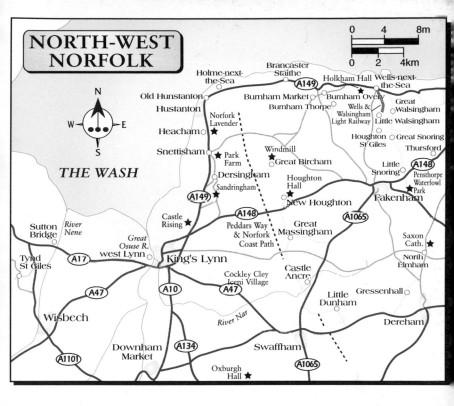

NORTH-WEST NORFOLK

Brancaster Staithe
Holme-next-the-Sea
Holkham Hall
Wells-next-the-Sea
A149
Old Hunstanton
Burnham Market
Burnham Overy
Great Walsingham
Hustanton
Burnham Thorpe
Wells & Walsingham Light Railway
Little Walsingham
Norfork Lavender
Heacham
Houghton St Giles
Great Snoring
Windmill
Thursford
Snettisham
Park Farm
Great Bircham
Little Snoring
A148
THE WASH
Dersingham
Houghton Hall
Penshorpe Waterfowl Park
Sandringham
New Houghton
Fakenham
A149
Sutton Bridge
River Nene
Castle Rising
A148
Peddars Way & Norfork Coast Path
Great Massingham
A1065
Saxon Cath.
Great Osuse R.
west Lynn
Tylud St Giles
A17
North Elmham
King's Lynn
Cockley Cley Iceni Village
Castle Ancre
A10
A47
Little Dunham
Gressenhall
A47
Wisbech
River Nar
Dereham
Downham Market
A134
Swaffham
A1101
Oxburgh Hall
A1065

and importance including two guildhalls, a custom house, and an array of merchants' houses along the medieval streets, some of which run down to the quays on the River Great Ouse.

The port is well placed for trade across the North Sea; from very early times there have been links with the Low Countries and Baltic ports, including the great Hanseatic League. Much cargo was transhipped for onward transport via the inland waterways to places such as Peterborough, Bedford and most of the Midlands.

The town hosted King John on his fateful last journey to Newark Castle, where he died not long after arrival. More famously, his baggage train misjudged the state of the tide in the Wash and was overtaken by the swiftly rising water, with great loss; optimists are said to be still hunting for the royal valuables.

The town centre is reasonably compact, with a pedestrianised High Street linking the two market places. At the north end is **Tuesday Market Place**, a large expanse with the old Duke's Head Hotel and the 19th century

Corn Exchange as the most eye catching buildings. The Corn Exchange has a comprehensive programme of music, craft fairs and similar events.

At the south end is the much more modest **Saturday Market Place**, close to **St Mary's parish church**, founded in 1101 as part of a Benedictine Priory. On the tower is a most unusual tidal clock.

Also at Saturday Market Place is the very attractive **Guildhall of the Holy Trinity** comprising four parts built at different times, the oldest in 1421. This part has a magnificent facade of chequerboard flint and stone. The guildhall houses a fine collection of historic civic regalia, including the exquisite 14th century 'King John's Cup'. Part of the complex is the **Old Gaol House Museum**, a 'spine-chilling experience' of the town's former gaol, well re-created, with a personal audio tour. Entrance is via the **Tourist Information Centre**, where a helpful 'Town Trail' leaflet can be obtained.

Just around the corner, in Queen Street, the **Town Museum of Lynn Life** has a most evocative display of domestic life through the centuries, including the earlier part of the 20th.

King Street-Queen Street is the other thoroughfare connecting the two market places. At the north end of King Street **St George's Guildhall**, the older of the two in the town, dating from about 1410, is the largest remaining 15th century guildhall in the country. This building has housed a wide range of activities over the centuries and is now the **Kings Lynn Centre for the Arts**.

The **Custom House** of 1683, perhaps the town's best known building, is by the side of the street at the end of an old quay.

Between St Mary's Church and South Quay is a former **Hanseatic warehouse** of 1425, now used as offices by Norfolk County Council.

Lynn Museum, with geological, archaeological and natural history displays, is situated in a former chapel, close to Old Market Street.

A little way to the north of the town centre is the suburb of North End, where the old fishermen's quarter of tightly packed cottages housed hundreds of families close to the dominant church of St Nicholas. As slum clearance of insanitary dwellings proceeded during the present century, the quarter was, inevitably, demolished. Surprisingly, two cottages in True's Yard have survived and have been refurbished and furnished in period as the basis of the **True's Yard Museum**, with additional buildings providing space for historic material concerning the fishing industry.

Kings Lynn has an ancient ferry, taking foot passengers at approximately 20 minute intervals across the River Great Ouse, Monday to Saturday.

Modern Kings Lynn has facilities consistent with a sizeable town and port, the centre of a considerable rural area – cinema, bowling arena, sports and leisure centres. From the railway station there are services direct to Cambridge and London, with connections at Ely to Peterborough (East Coast Main Line) and most parts of the Midlands.

Places to Visit: Kings Lynn

Old Gaol House Museum and Civic Regalia
Trinity Guildhall. Open Easter to end of October, daily 10.00 to 17.00. November to Easter, closed Wednesdays and Thursdays.
☎ 01553 763044.

True's Yard Museum
North Street. Tearoom with light refreshments all day. Open all year except Christmas Day, from 09.30, last admissions 15.45.
☎ 01553 765100.

Lynn Museum
Market Street. Open all year, Tuesday to Saturday, 10.00 to 17.00. Closed on public holidays. ☎ 01553 77500.

Town House Museum of Lynn Life
Queen Street. Open 2nd January to end of April, Monday to Saturday, 10.00 to 16.00; beginning of May to end of September, Monday to Saturday, 10.00 to 17.00; beginning of October to end of December, Monday to Saturday, 10.00 to 16.00. Closed on Bank Holidays.
☎ 01553 773450.

Strikes Bowling Arena
1-5 Lynn Road, Gaywood. Open 10.00 until late, every day. ☎ 01553 760333.

Skyride Balloons
Hot air balloon flights. Open 7 days a week.
☎ 07000 110210.

Caithness Crystal
Paxman Road, Hardwick Industrial Estate. Glassmaking centre and factory shop. Open 7 days a week, March to Christmas, 6 days during the rest of the year. Glassmaking Monday to Friday. ☎ 01553 76511.

Kings Lynn Sports Centre
Gaywood Road.
☎ 01553 760923.

Lynnsport
Green Park Avenue.
☎ 01553 777122.

of English Heritage, who provide an audio tour. The castle was owned from 1331 to 1358 by Queen Isabella, who was involved in the murder of her husband, King Edward II.

The red brick almshouses in the adjacent village were founded in 1614 and rebuilt 1807. There are long traditions including a special form of dress worn by the residents on ceremonial days.

Sandringham Estate has no village, but a great 7000 acre estate and country park owned by the Royal Family since 1862. During summer, several rooms of the great house, with surrounding grounds, an exhibition of royal cars and tearooms are open to the public if no member of the Royal Family is in residence.

Dersingham is a large village, with a pottery and art gallery in Chapel Road.

Along the Coast Road to Holme

The A149 leaves Kings Lynn to the north, heading alongside the Wash and serving a long section of the Norfolk coast.

Castle Rising is soon reached. This 12 acre (4.8 hectares) site has the strong and shapely keep of a Norman castle surrounded by huge earthworks, all in the care

Above: The Town House Museum, Kings Lynn
Below: The Queen's home at Sandringham

Snettisham has a coastal park and nature reserve reached by a long lane to Shepherd's Port, where there is provision for car parking. There are waymarked coastal walks up to 6km (3 miles) in length. To the east of the main road, Park Farm, with fun farmyard, red deer herd, adventure playground, craft workshops, tearoom and gift shop, is not far from the church.

Heacham sits between the main road and the sea. In the church is an alabaster relief of the Red Indian princess, Pocohontas, who married John Rolfe of Heacham Hall whilst he was in Virginia in 1614. Unfortunately, Pocohontas died at the age of 22, just three years later, leaving a son who later returned to America. Heacham Hall was destroyed by fire during World War II.

On the opposite (east) side of the main road, **Caley Mill** is prominently signposted. The mill is the centre of Norfolk Lavender, 'England's Lavender Farm', a large-scale lavender growing and marketing enterprise. The crop is picked during July and August, when visitors to the mill are offered tours of the fields and of the lavender water distillery barn at nearby Fring. A national collection of lavenders and a herb garden may also be seen.

A few miles to the east, at **Great Bircham** the fine windmill is a survivor of more than 300 such mills in Norfolk and claimed to be the only mill in working order which is open to the public. When possible the sails are used to turn the milling machinery. There is also a small bakery, 200 years old, with a coal-fired oven capable of baking 100 loaves at a time. The complex has cycle hire available, with advice on recommended local routes.

Hunstanton is a small, west-facing, seaside resort, with a compact shopping centre. Famous for its long cliff, rising immediately to the north of the centre, and its excellent beach, Hunstanton also has attractions such as pitch and putt and crazy golf in the clifftop gardens. Visitor facilities include the Oasis, an all-weather sea front leisure centre with swimming complex, Sea Life, with more than 30 displays, Jungle Wonderland, an adventure play area and the Princess Theatre.

Old Hunstanton has some attractive corners but is primarily residential, with a sea front golf course and the Le Strange Old Barns Antiques, Arts and Crafts Centre.

At the point where the coastline turns sharply to the east, Holme-next-the-Sea is a quiet village, largely by passed by the A149. A lane leads down towards the sea, with car parking, public conveniences and refreshments at the far end. A walking track leads across the golf course to the beach, less than 400m (400yds) distant. Holme is notable as the northern end of the ancient Peddars' Way long distance route.

Peddars Way

The Peddars Way is a very old route, certainly used by the Romans, but also very likely to pre-date the Roman conquest as a 'war road' of the Iceni tribe or as more mundane salt tracks. The Roman road was built immediately after AD61, following the great revolt of Boudicca and her Iceni tribesmen, for rapid troop movements, vital for keeping the tribesmen under control.

The generally straight alignment and the very substantial dimensions of the construction – up to 13.7 metres (45ft) in width and 760mm (2.25feet) thickness of the embankment (agger) in places confirm the military purpose.

The length traced is from Holme-next-the-Sea on the Norfolk coast to just south of Coney Weston in Suffolk, about 80km (50 miles), almost certainly linking with a ferry across the Wash at the north end. This gave a through route to Burgh-in-the-Marsh, Lincolnshire, and thence to the Roman garrison at Lincoln. There is a known Roman road between those places.

After the Roman departure, the Saxons had no real use for what was, to them, a rather mysterious historic highway leading to and from places beyond their experience. Consequently their villages were built away from the line of the road. Today, The Way comprises country lanes, waymarked bridleways and footpaths. It is all available to walkers and much of the distance is also used by horse riders. At Holme-next-the-Sea there is a link with the Norfolk Coast Path to provide a continuous National Trail of 150km (93 miles).

Despite the lack of villages, apart from Castle Acre and West Acre, there are interesting features along the Way. Swaffham, Great Bircham, Great and Little Massingham and Ringstead are not far from the direct line. Anmer Minque and Bircham Heath have round barrow burial mounds. The re-creation of an Iceni village at Cockley Cley is likewise accessible.

Peddars Way passes through countryside ranging from the heath of Breckland via the north-west Norfolk ridge to the dunes of the coast. There is a good deal of accommodation along the route and circular walks are being developed at several places, based on the Way. Booklets are also being published – enquire at Tourist Information Centres. Particular efforts will be made to ensure access to these routes by public transport, both bus and train.

Castle Rising Castle

Open from beginning of April to end of October, daily 10.00 to 18.00 (or dusk in October). November to end of March, Wednesday to Sunday, 10.00 to 16.00. Closed 24th to 26th Dec. ☎ 01553 631330.

Dersingham Pottery

Open daily all year, 10.00 to 17.30.

Park Farm

Snettisham
Gift shop and tearoom. Open daily from 10.00 to 17.30. ☎ 01485 542425 for winter opening hours.

Norfolk Lavender

Heacham. Plant centre with national collection of lavender, gift shop and tearoom. Open all year 9.30 to 17.00 (grounds, gift shop, plant centre). Tearoom open Easter to October, 10.00 to 17.00, November to Easter, 10.00 to 16.30. Guided tours: Spring Bank Holiday to end of September, 2-5 times daily. ☎ 01485 570384.

Old Barns Antiques, Arts and Crafts Centre

Old Hunstanton. Open summer 10.00 to 18.00, winter 10.00 to 17.00. ☎ 01485 533402.

Great Bircham Windmill

Gift shop, tearooms and cycle hire. Open daily from Easter to the end of September, 10.00 to 17.00. ☎ 01485 578393.

Oasis Leisure Centre

Hunstanton. Open from early February to late November. For public access times to pools, ☎ 01485 534227.

Sea Life

Hunstanton. Cafe and gift shop. Open daily from 10.00 in summer. ☎ 01485 533576 for winter opening details.

Jungle Wonderland

Hunstanton. Cafe and gift shop. For opening hours and times, ☎ 01485 535505.

Princess Theatre

Hunstanton. ☎ 01485 532252.

Sunny Hunny Sea Tours

☎ 01485 535455.

Villages Between Brancaster and Binham

Continuing along the A149 coast road, **Brancaster** is a pleasant red-roofed village, largely strung along the main road. There is a lane to a car park, public conveniences and a spacious sandy beach.

Brancaster Staithe, ('staithe' means landing place, quay) largely owned by the National Trust, is a waterside hamlet, with boating activity and a ferry (subject to the state of the tide) to Scolt Head Island, a large nature reserve. **Burnham Deepdale** has a roadside church with Saxon round tower.

Burnham Market is almost a small town, with spacious and attractive main street, inns, cafes and shops.

Burham Overy Town is close by, but the noted Burnham Overy Mill is almost 2km (1.25 mile) distant from the village, by the side of the A149.

Burnham Overy Staithe is another waterside community, by the side of a sea creek, with pleasure boating centre and a ferry (tide permitting) to Scolt Head Island, with its nature reserve. In past centuries Burnham Overy Staithe was a small port but progressive silting, coupled with the arrival of the railway to this area in 1866, ended the commercial use.

Burnham Thorpe is a rather scattered village, with a large green. It is the birthplace of Horatio (later Lord) Nelson. The actual house is long gone, but a well-signposted plaque on a wall almost 1km (0.5 mile) south of the village centre records the site.

Inside the church, where his father was Rector for many years, there is a bust of Nelson and several relevant flags from ships of the Royal Navy. During the years of naval inactivity, 1787 to 1793, Nelson lived in the area, no doubt eager to be back in action. He was very much a Norfolk man and his memory lives on, not only in the the obvious names of local inns, such as the 'Nelson' and the 'Hero', but by references to be found throughout East Anglia.

South from Burnham Market

The road to the south from Burnham Market soon reaches **North Creake** and **South Creake,** charming villages with flint-walled cottages and churches, so typical of this area. The church of Our Lady of St Mary at South Creake is particularly interesting. Despite the rigours of the Reformation, a rood screen and, more remarkably, statues including a Madonna, have survived. The church is high, light and bright, with a hammer beam roof. Both villages have tearooms, that at North Creake has a small museum displaying East Anglian bygones and a double forge.

• Lord Nelson •

Horatio (later Lord) Nelson, born at the Old Rectory, Burnham Thorpe in 1758, was very much a Norfolk man. His father was rector of Burnham Thorpe and three of the other Burnham parishes for no less than 46 years. The Old Rectory, which was demolished in 1803, stood at the far end of the village, almost 1km (600yds) from the church; the site is marked by a roadside plaque.

Inside the church Nelson's presence is felt very strongly indeed; the cross in the chancel arch and the lectern are both made from the timbers of *HMS Victory*, his flagship at the Battle of Trafalgar, where he met his death in 1805. The naval theme in the church continues with the crest of the World War II battleship *Nelson* and the flags of the World War I battlecruiser *Indomitable*. A marble bust of the great admiral is found on the wall above his father's tomb.

During the years 1787-93, when he was out of action 'beached', Nelson and his wife lived in Burnham Thorpe, leaving when he was offered command of the *Agamemnon*. Two years after his death, the Plough Inn was renamed the Lord Nelson.

His education gives the impression of having been spread all over Norfolk, from Downham Market to Norwich and North Walsham. At Norwich, the Old Grammar School, now the school chapel, was just inside the Erpingham Gate of the Cathedral; a marble statue of Nelson, with a telescope, is close by. At North Walsham he attended the Paston Grammar School from his tenth to his thirteenth year, leaving when his uncle was persuaded to take him on board his ship. The school still stands, on one side of the Market Square.

Those seeking out traces of Nelson will also visit the Guildhall in Norwich, where a Spanish Admiral's sword, presented by him to the city after the Battle of Cape St Vincent in 1797, is kept. On an unlikely and unattractive site in Great Yarmouth, behind the docks, a tall monument to Nelson, with the names of his four greatest battles, is crowned by the figure of Britannia.

Two kilometres (1.25 mile) north of North Creake are the remains of Creake Abbey, in the care of English Heritage. Originally a small hospital and almshouse for the poor, the Foundation became a Priory following the receipt of endowments. Promotion to Abbey status, of the Augustinian Order, was granted in 1231 by King Henry III.

Always few in number, the Canons were decimated by plague in the early 16th century, only the Abbott surviving. Consequent closure in 1506 predated King Henry VIII's general dissolution of the monasteries. The buildings were later used for farming purposes and as a house. The flint walling seen today is mainly of the 13th century, with some 15th century additions.

Holkham Hall is a large stately home occupied by seven generations of the Earls of Leicester. Open to the public are a grand entrance hall, magnificent state rooms and much else, including the old kitchen. Also on site are a separate Bygones Museum, gardens and deerpark, with a sizeable lake, pottery, gift shops, tearooms and restaurant.

Wells-next-the-Sea

Being next to the estuary nowadays, rather than next the sea, has not deterred Wells from carrying on as a minor port and fishing centre, with its attractive quay, narrow streets and some good Georgian houses by the green called the Buttlands. There is now a considerable presence of holiday visitors overlaying the original port activity, with a large caravan site connected to the quay by a waterside narrow gauge railway line and a busy little market. The Maritime Museum at the harbour side is well worth a visit.

The town has the northern terminus of the **Wells and Walsingham Light Railway**, a narrow gauge steam operated railway using the trackbed of the former British Rail line for 8km (5 miles) between the two places. The journey, across rolling countryside with cuttings rich in wild flowers and butterflies, takes about half an hour. The usual locomotive is a very fine purpose-built Garratt, 'Norfolk Hero' (Lord Nelson again!). Open and closed coaches cater for all types of weather.

Little Walsingham

Little Walsingham is a village of enormous historic and religious importance. It has been a centre of religious pilgrimage since the Virgin Mary appeared in a dream to the lady of the Manor in 1261.

On entering Little Walsingham the ruin of the Friary (no public access) is seen to the left. At the far end of High Street the ruins of the Abbey, founded in 1153 by Augustinian Canons, are to the right. The entrance is through the **Tourist Information Centre**,

The Forge Tearoom and Museum

North Creake. Open daily, 10.00 to 17.00.
☎ 01328 738910.

Holkham Hall

Stately home with gift shops, tearooms, restaurant, nursery gardens. House and Bygones Museum open late May to the end of September, Sundays to Thursdays, 13.00 to 17.00. Easter, May, Spring and Summer Bank Holidays, Sundays and Mondays, 11.30 to 17.00.

The Nursery Gardens are open every day except Christmas and Boxing Days, 10.00 to 17.00 (or dusk if earlier). Opening of the Stables restaurant and the pottery shop is generally similar to the house but extends through October and commences each day at 10.00. ☎ 01328 710227.

Maritime Museum

Wells-next-the-Sea. Open late March to late July, Tuesday to Friday, 14.00 to 17.00; Saturdays 10.00 to 13.00 and 14.00 to 17.00. Late July to beginning of September, daily 10.00 to 13.00, 14.00 to 17.00 and 18.00 to 20.00. September and October, Tuesday to Friday, 14.00 to 17.00, Saturday 10.00 to 13.00 and 14.00 to 17.00.
☎ 01328 711646.

Wells and Walsingham Light Railway

Wells-next-the-Sea. Open daily from Good Friday to the end of September.
☎ 01328 710631.

Courthouse Museum

Shirehall, Little Walsingham. Open from Easter to the end of October, Monday to Saturday, 10.00 to 16.30.
☎ 01328 820510.

Walsingham Abbey Grounds

Open all year. Entrance in summer months through Shirehall Museum and Tourist Information Centre,
☎ 01328 820510. Out of season, entrance through adjacent estate office,
☎ 01328 820259.

Great Walsingham Gallery

Textile centre with paintings, sculpture and craft demonstrations. Gift shop and coffee shop. Open Easter to Christmas, weekdays 09.30 to 17.00, Saturdays and Sundays 10.00 to 17.00. Christmas to Easter, Tuesday to Friday 09.30 to 17.00 Saturday 10.00 to 17.00. ☎ (textile centre) 01328 820009, (gallery) 01328 820900.

Binham Priory

Open at all reasonable times.
☎ 01604 230320.

• The Shrine at Walsingham •

Little Walsingham has been a place of pilgrimage since the Blessed Virgin appeared in a dream to Richeldis, Lady of the Manor of Walsingham in 1261. Richeldis established a shrine as a replica of the Holy House in Nazareth where the Angel Gabriel announced to Mary that she was to be the Mother of God.

It soon became the most important Marian shrine in Christendom, a place of pilgrimage until it was destroyed on the instructions of King Henry VIII following his break with the Roman Catholic Church. The religious history throughout the succeeding centuries has involved both Roman Catholics and Anglicans, with the re-commencement of pilgrimage in 1897.

The most appropriate route for a visit to Little Walsingham starts at the 'Slipper Chapel' near Houghton St Giles, where the 14th century chapel has been supplemented by modern buildings, forming the National Roman Catholic Shrine of Our Lady. At this chapel, medieval pilgrims would shed their shoes to walk barefoot for the last mile to the Shrine.

round the corner in Common Place.

A little further to the right, in Holt Road, is the modern (1931) **Anglican Shrine**, claiming to be 'England's Nazareth', beautifully set in gardens, with accommodation for pilgrims next door. To complete the overwhelming religious presence, there is also an impressive parish church, the only Georgian Methodist chapel (of 1794) still in use in East Anglia and a Russian Orthodox Chapel in the former railway station.

With or without a real interest in religious history, Little Walsingham is an attractive place for visitors, with timber framed buildings and Georgian facades. The modern visitor need not be any type of pilgrim to enjoy the inns, restaurants and tearooms which serve the village.

The southern terminus of the Wells and Walsingham Light Railway is close to the village centre.

Towards Binham

By contrast with its 'Little' namesake, **Great Walsingham** is quite an ordinary sort of place, pleasant but without distinction.

The parish church of St Peter is a good example of an unspoilt church of the Decorated period. The Great Walsingham Gallery, housed in a converted Norfolk barn with a lovely courtyard, has paintings, sculpture, textiles and demonstrations of traditional crafts.

Apart from their names, the charm of **Great Snoring** and **Little Snoring** lies in the flint cottages and a village sign which commemorates years of local Royal Air Force activity.

Binham has a Benedictine Priory founded in 1091. Always poor in comparison with most other monastic houses, Binham was dissolved in 1540. Now used as a parish church and for musical events throughout the summer, the surviving building has a magnificent west front with an Early English arch, rare in East Anglia. The ruins of the other Priory buildings are adjacent.

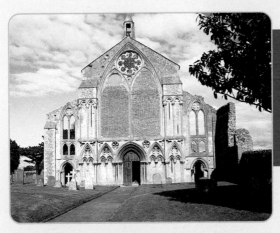

Above:
The Anglican Shrine at Little Walsingham

Left:
Binham Priory

Inland Villages and Market Towns

Thursford is known for its 'Collection', an extravaganza of restored road and agricultural steam engines and fairground organs, with catering, specialised shops, and daily performances on a Wurlitzer organ, all accommodated in an attractive complex.

Between Thursford and Fakenham, the **Old Barn Studios** at Kettlestone has fine art, with specialisation in bird and plant life and visiting artists for special exhibitions. Painting and drawing courses are held during the summer.

Fakenham is one of north Norfolk's largest market towns and a road communication centre for the area. The shopping centre, with supermarkets both in and out of town, is hugely complemented by the Thursday market which, coupled with the concurrent auction, covers much of the town centre.

Architecturally, the town centre is largely 18th century; it is well provided with inns and restaurants. National Hunt meetings are held on the racecourse at the edge of town which also has sufficient space to accommodate a large caravan site.

About 3km (2 miles) along the Norwich road, A1067, **Pensthorpe Water Park and Nature Reserve** claims to have the largest collection of waterfowl in Europe. The present visitor centre buildings were opened by the Duke of Edinburgh in 1988. The centre is very attractive, with audio-visual display, special exhibitions and a luxurious viewing gallery.

Some of the more unusual birds such as scarlet ibis, spoonbills and little egrets, are kept in enclosures, but the majority are unconfined, seen on or around the series of lakes created from former gravel workings, now beautifully landscaped. Waymarked trails with a suggested walking time of up to 2 hours thread their way through the extensive grounds. Buggies are provided for the less able.

A former Saxon cathedral is sited at **North Elmham**, between Fakenham and East Dereham. The timber building was the seat of the Bishop of East Anglia until 1071, when he moved to Thetford and, later, to Norwich. The cathedral became a parish church until about 1100, when it was replaced by a stone chapel for the private use of Bishop Herbert of Norwich. During the latter part of the 14th century it was converted to a castle for a later Bishop of Norwich. It fell into disuse in the 16th century and is now nothing more than a substantial ruin.

Gressenhall, close to East Dereham, has the **Norfolk Rural Life Museum** occupying a substantial former workhouse. A wide ranging collection of farming bygones, with reconstructed shops and workplaces displaying how people have lived and worked in Norfolk during the past 150 years or so comprises a major visitor attraction. The museum has ramps rather than steps, wheelchair loan and disabled facilities, gift shop and tearoom.

Close by, **Union Farm**, operated in conjunction with the museum, is stocked with rare breeds of cattle, sheep and pigs. There are woodland walks and a riverside trail.

East Dereham (or just Dereham) is one of the bigger agricultural centres and market towns of Norfolk. In fact there are two market days, large on Friday and small on Tuesday, complementing the generally good shopping facilities. Most of the town's buildings are later than the second of two great fires of the 16th and 17th centuries; understandably, 18th century facades now dominate.

The poet William Cowper, who died in 1800, is buried in the churchyard, with a window and a monument to his memory. **Bishop Bonner's Cottages** of 1502 are named after a 16th century rector who went on to become Bishop of London. The cottages, of brick, flint, wattle and daub construction, have ornamental plasterwork. An archaeological museum now occupies the cottages.

Dereham Mill, in Cherry Lane, just off the Norwich road, was built in 1836 as a brick tower corn mill with four sails and the usual fantail. The sails were removed in 1922, the stones now being driven by an external paraffin engine. Production finally ceased in 1937. Following several years of decay the building was purchased in 1979 by Breckland District Council and, over a period of eight years, the mill was restored as a landscape feature, but not to full working order.

Dereham Station is the headquarters of the volunteer group engaged in restoring a considerable length of the former Mid Norfolk Railway line. So far, about 18km (11 miles) of line between Dereham and Wymondham are back in use and there are ambitious plans to restore more line towards Fakenham.

The villages of **Little Dunham** and **Litcham** each have a museum. Dunham Museum has a collection of dairy, leathersmith and shoemaker's tools, bygones and machinery. Litcham Village Museum has artefacts from Roman times onwards, an underground lime kiln, and a photographic collection.

Swaffham is another attractive market town, compact, busy and a centre for the rural hinterland. There are plenty of shops, inns and cafes. The town clusters around the wedge-shaped Market Square, which has a notable domed and pillared butter cross. The statue on the top is of Ceres, goddess of agriculture. Also in the Market Square is the elegant former **Assembly Room** of 1817.

The church of St Peter and St Paul was renewed in the 15th century, with a 16th century tower and a newer delicate spire with a copper ball. Inside, the double hammer beam roof has 150 angels and richly moulded timbers.

Swaffham Museum is in the Town Hall, London Street, an 18th century building, formerly the house of a brewer. The museum has local history, temporary exhibitions and displays on prominent local figures such as W.E. Johns, the creator of fictional air ace, 'Biggles'.

The **EcoTech Centre** is an exciting modern environmental attraction with an innovative 'green' building, imaginative exhibitions and interactive displays.

Castle Acre is an attractive and historic village with a wealth of visitor interest, strategically sited at the point where the ancient Peddars' Way crosses the River Nar. William de Warenne, son in law of William the Conqueror, constructed a great motte (mound) crowned by a powerful flint keep. Most of the present village lies within what was the outer bailey of this castle.

Pass the huge church of St James to visit the remains of the great 11th century **Castle Acre Priory**, founded by the Cluniac Order and now owned by English Heritage. There is an informative visitor centre and, on the site proper, a glorious west front,

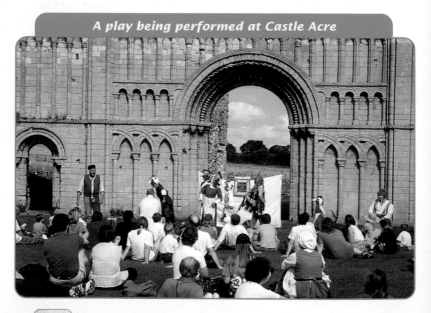

A play being performed at Castle Acre

Pensthorpe Waterfowl Park

decorated arches and the interesting and varied use of building materials, including flint, brick and two varieties of limestone - Caen and Barnack. The grounds of the Priory make a splendid venue for a summer programme of open air events, including 'medieval' fairs and entertainment.

Close by is West Acre, where the ruins of the Priory are not open to the public and are not easily seen from the public road. **West Acre Gardens** are situated less than 2km (1.25 mile) from the village. A 'plant lover's paradise', the gardens offer many unusual species.

Great Massingham has one of the largest village greens in Norfolk, divided by minor roadways and studded with ponds, some of them virtually lakes. Flint-built houses and the church of St Mary complete a lovely scene. Inside the church, the front of the high altar glows with the gold leaf finish on an intricate wood-carving of 1953.

Houghton Hall is a grand Palladian house built in the 1720s for Sir Robert Walpole, our first prime minister. James Gibbs was one of the architects and the interiors are by William Kent. It is privately owned and is the seat of the Marquess of Cholmondeley. Parts of the house are open to the public, as well as the walled garden, parkland with a large herd of white fallow deer, tearoom and gift shop. A specialised museum has the Cholmondeley collection of model soldiers, 20,000 of them, deployed in the representation of famous battles.

Thursford Collection

Tearooms. Open Good Friday to late October, 12.00 to 17.00.
☎ 01328 878477.

Museum of Gas and Local History

Hempton Road, Fakenham. Open high season only, Thursdays, 10.30 to 15.30.
☎ 01328 863150.

Fakenham Driving Range and Pitch and Putt course

Burnham Market Road. Open daily, 10.00 to 22.00.
☎ 01328 856614.

Old Barn Studios

Kettlestone. Open July, August, September and December, daily except Mondays, 11.00 to 17.30. January to Easter, daily except Mondays, Wednesdays and Thursdays, 14.00 to 16.30. Open on Bank Holidays. At other times, daily except Mondays, 14.00 to 17.00.
☎ 01328 878762.

Pensthorpe Waterfowl Park and Nature Reserve

Restaurant, countryside shop, adventure play area. Open daily from late March to early January. Weekends only from January to mid-March. Closed Christmas Day. Hours (late July to early September), 10.00 to 17.30. Other times, 11.00 to 16.00. ☎ 01328 851465.

Norfolk Rural Life Museum and Union Farm

Gressenhall. Tearoom, facilities for disabled people. Open from early April to the beginning of November, Monday to Saturday, 10.00 to 17.00, Sunday, 12.00 to 17.30. ☎ 01362 860563.

Dereham Windmill

Cherry Lane, Dereham. Open from mid-May to mid-September, Thursday to Sunday, 12.00 to 15.00.
☎ (Thetford Tourist Information Centre) 01842 752599.

Dereham Station

Headquarters for the restoration of the former Mid Norfolk Railway line; 18km (11 miles) between Dereham and Wymondham are in use. Souvenir shop, refreshments and toilets. Open when services are running.
☎ 01362 690633 for up to date information.

Swaffham Museum

Open from April to October, Tuesday to Saturday, 11.00 to 13.00 and 14.00 to 16.00.

Anglian Karting Centre

At the Activities Camp, 4km (2.5 miles) south-east of Swaffham on the North Pickenham road. Open from the beginning of April to the end of September, Wednesday 14.00 to 21.00;

Saturday, 13.00 to 18.00; Sunday, 12.30 to 18.00. Bank Holidays, 10.30 to 18.00. Also, most weekends in winter, Saturday 13.00 to 17.00, Sunday 12.30 to 17.00. ☎ 01760 441777.

Litcham Village Museum

'Fourways', Litcham. Open from early April to early October, Saturdays and Sundays, 14.00 to 17.00. ☎ 01328 701383.

Dunham Museum

Little Dunham. Open all year, Sundays, 10.00 to 17.00.

Castle Acre Priory

English Heritage. Open January to late March, Wednesday to Sunday, 10.00 to 16.00. Late March to the end of October, daily, 10.00 to 13.00 and 14.00 to 18.00

(or earlier dusk in October). November and December, Wednesday to Sunday, 10.00 to 16.00. Closed 24th to 26th December. ☎ 01760 755161.

West Acre Gardens

Open daily, March to mid-November, 10.00 to 17.00.

Houghton Hall

Near Kings Lynn. Tearoom and gift shop. Open from Easter to the end of September, Sundays, Thursdays and Bank Holiday Mondays, 14.00 to 17.30. ☎ 01485 528569.

Congham Hall Herb Gardens

Grimston. Open from April to the end of September, daily except Saturday, 14.00 to 16.00.

Walks: Kings Lynn

General guidance about walking in Norfolk as a whole, covering several chapters of this book in whole or in part, is included in a 'Norfolk Walks' package produced by the Planning and Transportation Department of Norfolk County Council, obtainable from Tourist Information Centres throughout the county. Some selected specimens of the kind of short walks typical of this area are included here.

1 Nar Valley Way

In addition to the greater part of the Peddars Way, this part of Norfolk also includes the Nar Valley Way, a route following the course of the River Nar for 54km (34 miles) from Kings Lynn to the Norfolk

Continued on page 58...

Continued...

Museum of Rural Life at Gressingham, near East Dereham, passing through West Acre and Castle Acre on the way.

The route follows public rights of way, tracks and minor roads, with plenty of intermediate car parking provision. Overnight accommodation is available at Castle Acre, about half way along the route.

2 Great Massingham

From Little Massingham, a short distance north of Great Massingham, drive along a very minor road past the church. In a little more than 1km (1100yds) park at a grassy triangle a little way past a road junction

Walk on for a few metres to a broad, unsurfaced lane and turn left. This lane is part of the famous Peddars Way; there are waymarks on a post. The Way rises very gently, almost but not quite straight, an ancient track beside fields of corn. In less than 1km (1100yds) turn left at a junction; there is a waymarked post.

The new track is similar to the Peddars Way, heading for communications masts and Great Massingham. Close to the masts, the track becomes a concrete roadway, bordered by cornfields. Ox eye daisies, field edge poppies and bindweed add a little colour.

The edge of Great Massingham soon comes into view. Join a minor public road (if time is pressing there is a sharp left turn along a surfaced lane here which will bring you back to the parking place in not much more than 1 km) However, it would be a shame not to continue into Great Massingham.

Turn right along the public road, soon reaching the northern edge of the largest of the several village ponds. To explore this spacious and attractive village turn right towards the church, the Rose and Crown Inn and the post office and village stores.

The best return route is to retrace steps along the minor road, passing the point at which our track joined, and then bearing right; this is the lane recommended above as a short cut. The overall distance, including exploring Great Massingham, is about 5km (3 miles).

A little longer and much more adventurous return can be made by using footpaths which start to the north of the village. Turn left off the Little Massingham road, into Sunnyside, then through a gate. The path is rather vague. Continue to a junction of paths, through more gates and close to a fence on the left.

The path continues in a fairly straight line along the edge of a cultivated field, becoming more overgrown until eventually a way has to be forced through the undergrowth by a tree belt to reach a cornfield.

Go across or round the right hand edge of the field to a strip of trees on the far side, where there is a good path among the trees. Turn right to walk to a minor road, where there is a farm almost opposite. Turn left to return to the parking place in less than 0.5km (550yds).

↑3 Castle Acre

Park in the village centre and walk on along Priory Road, with the large church on the left. (At a T-junction turn left by the public conveniences to make a visit to the Priory). Otherwise, turn right at the junction, then left in 60m (65 yds). at a 'Nar Valley Way' signpost to go along a stoney surfaced lane. After a right hand bend turn left in approximately 200m (220 yds) through a waymarked kissing gate.

Medieval crafts on display at Castle Acre

Continued on page 60...

Continued...

A good grassy path keeps close to the modest River Nar for some distance until the woodland of the West Acre Estate is entered at a kissing gate. Squirrels and pheasants may be seen here. Leave the wood at an old iron gate to cross a rough meadow.

Go over a stream on a wooden footbridge. The large house to the left is Mill House. Cross another footbridge over the River Nar to reach a public road.

Turn right towards a ford and footbridge, but turn left immediately before the bridge to follow a clear footpath, at first quite close to the river. The way is clear; as the tracks divide keep to the wider. Join a more important track, turning sharp left, then right in a further 10m. (To visit West Acre village, turn right along the more important track and cross the river by the footbridge).

After the right turn follow a waymarked path along the edge of a field. Go straight across the public road to a broad, sandy, agricultural track with signpost, slightly uphill. Pass the end of a tree belt, still rising.

As the track bends sharply to the right, turn left along a waymarked 'road used as public path' along the bottom edge of a field, now almost level. Go straight across a junction. The fields have crops of sugar beet, with some wheat, enlivened by the colour of field-edge poppies and ox eye daisies, with busy butterflies.

Turn left at the next junction to pass an isolated house before reaching a large farm complex. As a wide driveway sweeps to the right into the farm, go straight on here to join the road, Turn right for about 400m (440yds); over a gate on the left of the road part of an ancient moat can be seen.

Pass the flint church of St George, South Acre. Fork left at 'Ford, unsuitable for motors', then left again to pass a house called 'Little Brooms'. Continue along an unsurfaced lane, with glimpses of the ruin of Castle Acre Priory.

Cross the river by the footbridge at a pretty spot, then rise along the surfaced road towards Castle Acre village. Reach the church, then turn right, back to the village centre.

Without diversion, about 10km (6 miles) in length.

North-west Norfolk is a splendid area for cyclists. There are no great hills but most of the countryside is sufficiently undulating to give the interest of frequently changing views over farming land, well dotted with towns and villages. There is also the coastal strip with some of its nature reserves readily reached on two wheels.

Most of this area is well provided with minor roads, quiet lanes for the most part, very suitable for cycling. Many of the visitor attractions which provide the destination for a day out are well away from major centres of population and busy roads.

The **Norfolk Coast Cycleway** from Kings Lynn to Cromer is the subject of a leaflet obtainable at Tourist Information Centres. A map-guide with full detail is available from the Tourist Information Centre at Cromer ☎ 01263 512497.

The **Wensum Valley** (running between Fakenham and Norwich) and adjacent area has well organised routes throughout its length, from close to Norwich to the villages of Raynham and Rudham. Excellent leaflets at very small cost include the actual routes, places of interest, suggestions for accommodation and useful addresses and telephone numbers.

Norfolk Cycling Holidays offer a complete holiday package, including accommodation, maps, and pre-planned routes for most of the county. ☎ 01485 540642.

Windmill Ways Walking and Cycling Holidays provide for walking or cycling without having to carry luggage.
☎ 01603 871111.

Above: The dramatic cliffs at Hunstanton
Below: The Red Lion Inn, Swaffham

A drive along the coast is the most obvious excursion in this part of Norfolk. The A149 provides the connection between Kings Lynn, Castle Rising, Sandringham, Hunstanton, Brancaster, Burnham Market and Wells-next-the-Sea. The obvious return for a circular excursion is via Fakenham and the A148.

Add the odd stately home or windmill and there is more than enough for several days out.

To continue along the coast to Blakeney, Sheringham and Cromer, returning inland by Felbrigg, Blickling, North Aylsham, is still well within reach.

From Kings Lynn or nearby places, the destinations in Lincolnshire mentioned in Chapter 1 are easily accessible. Likewise, Peterborough, Huntingdon, Bedford and Cambridge are all well within the reach of motorists from any base in north Norfolk. Norwich is almost an obligatory destination from bases in at least the first five chapters in this book. The city can readily be combined with, say, the Norfolk Broads but there is so much of interest for whole families that it really does merit a day to itself.

Additional Information

Hotels

Kings Lynn

The Duke's Head
☎ 01553 774996 Fax 763556

Knight's Hill Hotel,
South Wootton
☎ 011553 675566

Butterfly Hotel
☎ 01553 771707 Fax 768027

**Congham Hall
Country House Hotel**,
Grimston ☎ 01485 600250

Burnham Market

The Hoste Arms
☎ 01328 738777 Fax 730103

Swaffham

The George Hotel
☎ 01760 721238

Stratton House
In town centre but country house style hotel ☎ 01760 723845 Fax 720458

Hunstanton

LeStrange Arms Hotel
☎ 01485 534411 Fax 534724

The Linksway
Country House Hotel,
Old Hunstanton
☎ and Fax 01485 532209

The Golden Lion
☎ 01485 532688 Fax 535310

Guest Houses and B&B

Kings Lynn

Fairlight Lodge,
79 Goodwins Road
☎ 01553 770280

The Old Rectory,
33 Goodwins Road
☎ 01553 768544

Marsh Farm,
Wolferton ☎ 01485 540265

East Dereham

Peacock House,
Old Beetley
☎ 01362 860371

Hunstanton

Fieldsend,
Homefields Road
☎ and Fax 01485 532593

The Oriel Lodge,
Homefields Road
☎ 01485 532368 Fax 535737

Self-catering

Hunstanton

Belle Vue Apartments
☎ 01485 532826
(day) 532156 (eve)

Nr Swaffham

Hall Barn Cottages,
Beachamwell
☎ 01366 328794

North Elmham

The Watermill,
7 apartments
☎ 01362 668928 Fax 668019

Caravan and Camping Sites

Near Kings Lynn

Bank Farm Caravan Park,
Saddlebow ☎ 01553 617305

Pentney Park Caravan Site,
Narborough ☎ 01760 337479

Sandringham

**Sandringham Estate
Caravan Site** (no tents)
☎ 01553 631614

Eating Out

Kings Lynn

**Phinns Restaurant and
Bistro**, Tower Street
☎ 01553 767887

The Orangery,
Congham Hall, Grimston
Award winning restaurant
☎ 01485 600250

Burnham Market

The Hoste Arms,
restaurant also bar meals
☎ 01328 738777

Castle Acre

Willow Cottage Tearooms
☎ 01760 755551

Sandringham

Restaurant and tearoom
at the visitor centre

Great Bircham

The Mill Tearoom

Public Transport

Railway services are restricted to the line which runs from London, Cambridge and Ely to Kings Lynn, the 'Fen Line', most of which is outside the scope of this chapter. The service to London is generally hourly.

Bus services cover the principal towns and many villages. There is a service (no.780) between Lowestoft and Kings Lynn, twice daily for most of its length.

A **'Coastliner Tour'** operates from late May to late September on Tuesdays, Wednesdays, Thursdays and Bank Holidays over much of this route. 'Day Ranger', 'Sunday Rover' and 'Three Day Ranger' special tickets are available.

The Sunday Rover gives all day travel on many routes throughout East Anglia as a whole for a very reasonable price. Discounts on admission charges to holders of Sunday Rover tickets are offered at many visitor attractions.

For all bus services in Norfolk, ☎ Norfolk Bus Information Centre, Freecall 0500 626116 (not Sunday) for details.

3 SHERINGHAM, CROMER & NORTH-EAST NORFOLK

North-east Norfolk is deservedly a popular holiday area, with its fine coastline backed in many places by low cliffs and with higher ground inland, including Norfolk's highest point at Beacon Hill. The Victorian holiday resorts of Sheringham and Cromer have retained much of their popularity.

Quite different is the coast at Blakeney and Cley-next-the-Sea. The attraction here is of an altogether quieter nature, with both fresh and salt marshes and seal colonies at Blakeney Point. Much of the coast has been designated as an Area of Outstanding Natural Beauty.

Inland the towns, largely set in rolling countryside, are varied and attractive, with evidence of the wool trade history at places such as Worstead. Major visitor centres, including the National Trust stately homes at Blickland and Fellbrigg, add to the overall interest of this area. The

Above: The pier, Cromer

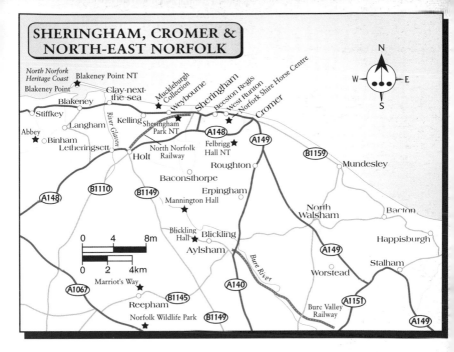

SHERINGHAM, CROMER & NORTH-EAST NORFOLK

itinerary-based information set out below starts and finishes at the coast.

Sheringham

Founded on a historic fishing village, **Sheringham** is a 19th century seaside resort, largely of Victorian and Edwardian buildings. The seafaring tradition now survives mainly in the manning of the lifeboat.

The clean washed sandy beach is a great attraction, supplemented by a leisure pool, museum and various other visitor facilities. The **Little Theatre** opens from May to September, with a programme which includes films and theatrical productions.

The **North Norfolk Railway** is a mainly steam operated preserved line, using the trackbed of part of the former British Rail branch between Sheringham and Holt, with an intermediate stop at Weybourne. Originally this line was a part of the Midland and Great Northern Joint Railway.

At Sheringham, the station area has static exhibits, shop and buffet. Rather more unusually, tuition in driving a steam locomotive is on offer. The line winds around the end of the wooded hill behind the town and is scenically attractive. There is a service, much reduced out of season, during each month other than January. Two former 'Brighton

Belle' Pullman restaurant coaches are used for serving special meals.

Sheringham has plentiful shopping facilities, busy roads and streets and, arguably, more than enough informal catering. There is a railway, the 'Bittern Line', with an approximately hourly service to and from Norwich and the town is on the Norfolk Coastliner bus route (see Public Transport, Chapter 2).

Behind Sheringham is a ridge of wooded land, high by East Anglian standards, where Upper Sheringham is a separate village. **Sheringham Park**, designed in 1812 by Humphrey Repton, the great landscape gardener, is now owned by the National Trust. From the park there are spectacular views of coast and countryside, magnificent rhododendrons, viewing towers and walks. Very occasionally, at some Bank Holidays, a restored 1920s steam powered sawmill is operated. Pretty Corner has a car park.

From Sheringham to Cromer

At Beeston Regis, on the eastern edge of Sheringham, **Priory Maze** has attractive wild flower meadow, ponds and stream and wildlife all adding to the attraction of the maze itself. Just beyond Weybourne, the **Muckleburgh Collection** claims to be Britain's largest working military collection, privately owned and all under cover. Tank demon-

Fellbrigg

A short diversion inland, close to Roughton, the Jacobean mansion of **Fellbrigg** has been growing gradually over more than three centuries. It is now owned by the National Trust, but before that, four generations of the Windham family and their successors accumulated furniture, books and pictures to fill its beautiful rooms.

'Grand tour' paintings and ornate plasterwork are particular features. A walled garden of almost 1.2 hec (3 acres), with octagonal dovehouse, is the highlight of the gardens, which are surrounded by a spacious park, largely wooded, and with several designated trails. Facilities include the Park Restaurant, the Turret Tearoom, picnic area, shop and bookshop. All ground floor facilities are accessible to wheelchair users; wheelchairs are freely available.

strations are given on Sundays and Bank Holiday Mondays; also on weekdays during school summer holidays.

West Runton is soon reached, where the **Norfolk Shire Horse Centre** has also the 'Countryside Collection' of farming bygones and a Children's Farm. Working demonstrations of such crafts as harnessing are given and there are cart rides for children, a video show and an indoor area for wet weather demonstrations. There is a riding school adjacent to the centre.

Cromer

The 'other' seaside holiday resort of the North Norfolk Coast, Cromer has long been famous for its sea fishing, with crabs the speciality.

Like all good seaside resorts, the popularity of Cromer is founded on its fine beach, supplemented by the visitor attractions such as the **pier with its theatre**, which has a programme of summer shows, and the **museum**, housed in a row of tiny fishermen's cottages beside the church, exhibiting much local material and a reconstituted Victorian fisherman's cottage. There is also a **Lifeboat Museum**.

In addition to the profusion of shops, cafes and restaurants, Cromer does have a small old town, with narrow streets pressing close to the church of St Peter and St Paul. The church tower, at 49m (160ft) is the highest in Norfolk. The town is served by the Bittern Line railway to Sheringham and Norwich and by the Coastliner bus service.

Behind Cromer two designated **footpaths,** the Norfolk Coast **Path and The Weavers'** Way join together.

Places to Visit
In & Around Sheringham & Cromer

North Norfolk Railway

Preserved railway line to Holt. Services each month other than January. Mainly steam-hauled trains. ☎ 01263 822045 (office hours) 01263 822972 (other times).

Sheringham Little Theatre

Performances from early May to late September.

☎ 01263 822347 (box office).

Priory Maze and Gardens

Beeston Regis. Open from mid-June to mid-September, Sundays and Wednesdays, 11.00 to 17.00.
☎ 01263 822986.

Continued on page 70...

Norfolk Shire Horse Centre

West Runton. Facilities for the disabled. Open March to October, daily except Saturdays (open on Saturdays during June, July, August), 10.00 to 17.00.
☎ 01263 837339.

The Muckleburgh Collection of Military Vehicles

Weybourne. Working demonstrations. Facilities for the disabled. Open from mid-Feb to November, 10.00 to 17.00.
☎ 01263 588210.

Cromer Museum

Shop. Open daily, Monday to Saturday, 10.00 to 17.00 (closed Mondays 13.00 to 14.00). Sundays 14.00 to 17.00.

Pavilion Theatre, Cromer

Seaside variety shows. Open from mid-June to mid-September. ☎ 01263 512495.

Fellbrigg Hall

National Trust house, gardens and park. Shop and refreshments. Facilities for the disabled. Open (Hall and gardens) from end of March to the beginning of November, daily except Thursdays and Fridays, (hall) 13.00 to 17.00, (gardens) 11.00 to 18.00, (estate) dawn to dusk every day except Christmas Day. ☎ 01263 837444.

Fellbrigg Hall

Mundesley, North Walsham and Reepham

Next along the coast (the road now being the B1159) is **Mundesley**, an altogether different sort of place, quiet and discreet, a former fishing hamlet catering for much smaller numbers of visitors. The hamlet has a modern overlay and is now a large village with an excellent sandy beach backed by floral decorations and a mini-golf course.

Also close to the beach is a much restored church and a tiny **Maritime Museum**, operated on a voluntary basis. A little way inland is a useful range of shops.

After Mundesley a long stretch of the coastline is relatively undistinguished, with a large oil terminal close to Bacton. **Happisburgh** has good access to the sea, with a safe bathing beach. The 15th century church, with its tower visible from well out to sea, and also a lighthouse, both contribute as aids to navigation.

Turning inland for a few kilometres, **North Walsham** is a pleasant small market town, with a distinctive market cross of 1549, subsequently damaged and restored. Nelson attended Paston Grammar School for three years. The school is still here, but has been rebuilt since Nelson's day. The large parish church of St Nicholas, mainly 14th century, has the dubious distinction of a

The former railway station at Reepham and its display of produce for sale

ruined tower. There is an elaborate porch with statues; inside are fine arcades, a massively ornamental font cover, an impressive organ and much more.

The town has plenty of individual shops and, much more unusually, a Conservation Award-winning Woolworth's store in a converted inn. **The Motor Cycle Museum**, close to the railway station, has more than 60 motorcycles dating from the 1920s to the 1960s. There is a railway service to and from Norwich, Cromer and Sheringham on the 'Bittern Line'. Thursday is market day.

Worstead may be small but it is certainly significant, having given its name to a finely woven woollen cloth (worsted) well known throughout Britain for centuries.

The industry was founded by immigrant Flemish weavers in Norman times and their lasting monument is the great church which they erected in the 14th century, truly a 'wool church'. The large nave has a hammer beam roof, great screens and a fine font cover among the internal features. In Church Plain, close by, there several 17th century weavers' houses.

The **Dinosaur Adventure Park** is close to the A1067 at Lenwade, south of Reepham, quite a distance across country from Worstead. Here, one of the world's largest collection of life size dinosaurs can be seen, spread throughout acres of woodland. The models are complemented by an adventure play area, crazy golf, refreshments and picnic area. About 5km(3 miles) further along the main road.

The **Norfolk Wildlife Park** at Great Witchingham has a good array of animals, for the most part housed in quite spacious paddocks in 40 acres of parkland. Included are reindeer, lynx, barbary apes and birds of prey, with the emphasis on native species, also a model farm, with rare domestic breeds of farm animal. Visitor facilities include a tearoom and gift shop.

Marriott's Way

At the former Reepham Station there is a small museum, tea and coffee room and a gift shop coupled with a substantial cycle hire depot. Thirty-four kilometres (21 miles) of the trackbed of the former railway line have been made available as a rural trail for walkers, cyclists and horse riders.

This route has been designated 'Marriott's Way' in memory of William Marriott, chief engineer of the former Midland and Great Northern Joint Railway for 41 years. The Way is made up of parts of the M&GN and the Great Eastern Railways. There is a link with the Riverside Path at the Norwich end of the line, increasing the length of the route by a further 8km (5 miles). For walkers there is also a link with the 'Weavers' Way' long distance footpath and with the Bure Valley Walk at Aylsham.

Reepham is one of the smaller towns of the area, now less important than it was in the 18th century, when it had a market and was the centre of a barley growing and brewing district. The old market place has some attractive buildings, including the Kings Arms Inn, with a notably Dutch/Flemish influence.

The churchyard once had no less than three churches within its compass. One has been a ruin since 1543, only a fragment now remaining, but St Michael's, the church of neighbouring Whitwell parish, still stands back to back with St Mary's, the parish church of Reepham, a curious arrangement. The latter church has an unusual Norman font.

Places to Visit: In & Around
Mundesley, North Walsham & Reepham

**Mundesley
Maritime Museum**

Operated by volunteers. Open from May to September, Thursdays and Saturdays, 10.00 to 16.00, other days, including Sundays, 10.00 to 15.00.

Dinosaur Adventure Park

Lenwade off the A1067 south of Reepham. Adventure play areas, crazy golf, refreshments, picnic area. Open April to August, daily from 10.00. Sept, restricted opening ☎ 01603 870245.

**Norfolk
Motorcycle Museum**

North Walsham. Open daily 10.00 to 16.30. Closed on Sundays from October to Easter.
☎ 01692 406266.

Norfolk Wildlife Centre and Country Park

Great Witchingham, 2km (1.25 miles) from Lenwade on A1067 road. Adventure play area, tearoom, gift shop and picnic areas. Open April to October, daily, 10.30 to 18.00.

Reepham Station

Cycle hire (not in winter), Marriott's Way and refreshments. Shop and shop museum. Open from 10.00 to 17.00 except at Christmas and New Year.
☎ 01603 871187.

• Weavers' Way •

This long distance footpath runs for 92km (57 miles) from Cromer to Great Yarmouth. The name comes from the ancient weaving industry. Particular centres were Aylsham, North Walsham, Stalham and Worstead. Scenically the route is well varied, with the rich farmland and the woodland of North Norfolk contrasting with the grazing marshes of the Norfolk Broads.

The National Trust estates of Fellbrigg and Blickling are *en route* and, from Aylsham to Stalham, the trackbed of the former Great Yarmouth to King's Lynn railway line is incorporated. The Broads section of the route passes through Hickling Broad National Nature Reserve and Breydon Water Local Nature Reserve on its way to Great Yarmouth. Here it joins the Angles Way, which runs almost to Thetford. By following Angles Way, then using Peddars' Way to connect with the Norfolk Coast Path at Holme-next-the-Sea, an enormous circuit can be achieved.

Aylsham to Cley

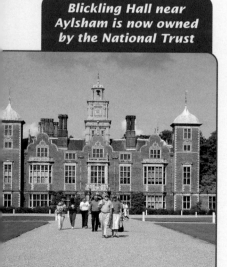

Blickling Hall near Aylsham is now owned by the National Trust

Aylsham is a small market town with well varied architecture and many individual shops around its largely red brick Market Place. Until the Industrial Revolution, the town was a considerable woollen centre.

The Millgate area was formerly a small port on the River Bure, trading with Norwich and Great Yarmouth, but flooding and the arrival of the railways put an end to this trade and the 18th century buildings are now in residential use. Markets are held on Mondays (with auction), Tuesdays and Fridays.

The **Bure Valley Railway** is a major attraction, its 15 inch gauge line running for 14.5km (9 miles) between Aylsham and Wroxham, mainly steam operated by

The Ghost of Anne Boleyn

There is a legend that Anne Boleyn was born and grew up in an earlier house on the site of Blickling Hall and that her ghost returns to Blickling each year on the anniversary of her execution.

attractive little locomotives. There are intermediate stations at Brampton, Buxton and Coltishall. The main depot is at Aylsham, where museum, model railway, tourist information, shop, restaurant and picnic area are available to visitors. Services run from April to October, with special events throughout the season.

A short distance to the northwest of Aylsham, along the B1354, **Blickling Hall** is a flagship property of the National Trust in East Anglia. The house, built between 1616 to 1624, is beautifully symmetrical, with red brick Jacobean facade and numerous interesting architectural features, particularly the chimneys, all set between an approach way of great yew hedges

Inside the house there is a wonderful plaster ceiling in the long gallery, a collection of furniture of the 18th and 19th centuries and an extensive library.

The extensive grounds of nearly 5000 acres include formal gardens, parkland and lake, all available to visitors for walks, short and not so short. Facilities are comprehensive – shop, restaurant and tearoom, plant sales.

Heading north along the A140 towards Cromer leads to **Alby Crafts**, by the side of the main road, close to Erpingham village. Alby is a working craft centre, promoting mainly British, including much East Anglian, craftsmanship.

Set inside restored farm buildings are a bottle museum, paintings, sculpture and ceramics, whilst a 'plantsman's garden' offers 4 acres of ponds, unusual shrubs, plants and bulbs. A tearoom provides drinks and light meals throughout the day. A more unusual attraction is the **Norfolk Children's Book Centre**, a little way further north, by the side of a lane a short distance to the west of the main road. Situated close together.

Mannington and **Wolterton** are both stately homes at the smaller end of the scale, family properties of the estate owned by Lord and Lady Walpole, descended from the brother of Britain's first prime minister. Neither house is normally open to the public, but Wolterton has guided tours on four days each year and parties are accepted by prior arrangement. There is entry to a small visitor centre, gardens, park, shop and tearoom at Mannington and to the parkland at Wolterton. A 'Conservation Trail and Walks Map' is available at Mannington.

Further to the north-west is **Baconsthorpe Castle**, the ruin of a 15th century part moated, semi-fortified house. Remaining are inner and outer gatehouses and curtain wall.

At Kelling, the **East Anglian Falconry Centre** claims to be the largest in the country, a National Sanctuary, with more than 200 birds of prey, including some rarer species. There are daily flying display; weather permitting. Facilities include play area, cafe and gift shop.

Holt

Without doubt one of the nicest towns in Norfolk, Holt is no longer a market town but still bustling, its streets, alleys and courtyards well packed with shops, inns and cafes. A great fire in 1708 destroyed much of the town, hence the predominance of Georgian buildings.

Just outside the town, **Holt Country Park** is a survival of an old heathland area, with a small visitor centre, car parking and walks along waymarked trails.

Holt station on the edge of town is the terminus of the North Norfolk preserved railway line, with mainly steam hauled trains to Sheringham (for more details refer to 'Sheringham').

About 2km (1.25 mile) along the main road to the west from Holt is **Letheringsett Watermill**, still producing wholewheat flour from locally grown wheat. The present mill was built in 1802 on a very ancient mill site and was restored to use in 1982. Working demonstration are given on most days. Flour is available for purchase at the mill and there is also a gift shop.

A little further north along the valley of the River Glaven, the **Natural Surroundings Wild Flower Centre** has 10 acres devoted to wild flowers and the traditional British countryside, with gardens and nature trail. A small visitor centre also has a shop, plant sales and tearoom.

A lane to the west leads to **Langham**, where Langham Glass is housed in a complex of 18th century Norfolk barns. Glassblowers using traditional tools can be seen at work. Among other attractions are an enclosed children's adventure playground, walled garden, factory gift shops, museum and restaurant.

Blakeney

The coast can be rejoined at the pleasant village of Stiffkey or, by bearing more to the right, to **Blakeney**, a little town and former port with an atmosphere all of its own, undoubtedly one of Norfolk's showpieces. The sea has receded over the centuries leaving a network of creeks threading their way through the huge marshes, both salt and freshwater.

The marshes separate the town from distant **Blakeney Point**, where a nature reserve owned by the National Trust is a prime site for viewing seals, birds and wild flowers. Blakeney boatmen compete to provide one hour trips to the Point when the tide is sufficiently high.

Inland are narrow streets, with flower-girt courts and alleyways separating the cottages, a mixture of flint and colour washed rendered walls. The church of St Nicholas stands massively on its inland hilltop site, with 15th century towers. Inside, there is a lovely old hammerbeam roof, graced with angels, and a soaring arch. The old Guildhall, facing the Quay, is built of Flemish bricks. The undercroft has brick vaulting more than 600 years old.

The nearby village of **Cley-next-the-Sea**, like Wells no longer really qualifies for its name. It is still a place of considerable charm, with an early 18th century tower mill, which ground corn until 1918, facing the distant sea. At Cley Marshes the coastal nature reserve is the oldest in the country operated by the Wildlife Trust. The visitor centre has a small display and shop. There is a beach cafe close by.

Places to Visit
Aylsham to Cley

Bure Valley Railway

Aylsham. Narrow gauge, mainly steam hauled railway line. museum, model railway, restaurant, picnic area, shop, tourist information. Services operate from April to October (only during school half-term holiday in October).
☎ 01263 733858.

Blickling Hall

National Trust, stately home. Gardens, shop, restaurant and tearoom. Open (house) from early April to July, Wednesday to Sunday and Bank Holiday Mondays, 13.00 to 16.30. August, Tuesday to Sunday and Bank Holiday Mondays, 13.00 to 16.30. September to the beginning of November, Wednesday to Sunday, 13.00 to 16.30. Garden: same days as house, 10.30 to 17.30, daily during August; September to March, Sundays only, 11.00 to 16.00. Park and woods daily all year, dawn to dusk.
☎ 01263 733084.

Alby Crafts

A140 close to Erpingham. Craft centre, gardens, gift shop and tearoom. Open from mid-March to mid-December, Tuesday to Sunday and Bank Holidays. Weekends only, mid-January to mid-March, 10.00 to 17.00.
☎ 01263 761590.

Norfolk Children's Book Centre

Close by Alby Crafts. Open Monday to Saturday, 10.00 to 17.00, closed Bank Holidays.
☎ 01263 761402.

Wolterton Park

Grounds of stately home and visitor centre with information display and toilets. Open every day from 09.00 to dusk. ☎ 01263 584175.

Mannington Gardens

Gardens of stately home and surrounding estate land. Tearooms. Open from late May to end of August, Wednesdays, Thursdays and Fridays. May to September, Sundays only. 12.00 to 17.00. ☎ 01263 584175.

Baconsthorpe Castle

Castle ruins. Open daily from 10.00 to 16.00.

East Anglian Falconry Centre

Kelling. Play area, cafe and gift shop. Open daily in summer, 10.00 to 17.00. Winter (October to March), weekends only, 10.00 to 15.00.

North Norfolk Railway

Holt. Mainly steam hauled preserved railway line. Refer to Sheringham for details.

Letheringsett Watermill

Flour milling demonstrations and shop. Open all year. Whitsun to early September, Tuesday to Saturday, 09.00 to 13.00, 14.00 to 17.00. Late July to early September, Sundays and Bank Holidays, 14.00 to 17.00. September to Whitsun, Tuesday to Friday, 09.00 to 13.00 and 14.00 to 17.00. Saturday, 09.00 to 13.00. ☎ 01263 713153.

Natural Surroundings Wild Flower Centre

North of Letheringsett. Plant sales, cafe and gift shop. Open from the end of March to early October, Tuesday to Sunday, 10.00 to 17.30. Rest of year (except Christmas week), Thursday to Sunday, 10.00 to 16.00. Open all Bank Holidays, 10.00 to 17.30. ☎ 01263 711091.

The Bure Valley Railway at Aylsham

Langham Glass

Langham, B1156. Glassblowing demonstrations, museum with video, adventure playground, shop and restaurant. Open all year, 7 days a week, 10.00 to 17.00, except over Christmas. ☎ 01328 830511.

Blakeney Point Nature Reserve

Boat trips from Blakeney or Morston, particularly for seal viewing. ☎ 01263 740038 (Morston Quay). ☎ 01263 740791 (Blakeney Quay).

Blakeney Guildhall

Open at any reasonable time. ☎ 01604 730320.

Cley Mill

Open daily from late March to the beginning of November, 14.00 to 17.00. ☎ 01263 740209.

Cley Marshes Nature Reserve

Visitor centre. Gift shop and refreshments. Disabled access. Open daily (closed Mondays other than Bank Holidays). Visitor centre open April to October, 10.00 to 17.00. ☎ 01263 740008.

There is no lack of opportunity in this diverse area. The Norfolk Coast Path connects with the Peddars Way (see Chapter 2) at Holme-next-the-Sea and the Weavers' Way near Cromer. Several lengths of the Coast Path can readily be incorporated into shorter circular walks. See below for example.

Many parishes have organised walks within their particular locality, collated by Norfolk County Council in their 'Norfolk Walks' pack of leaflets.

1 Mannington Estate

Start from the front of the visitor centre by going along a welcoming grass track towards trees. There are waymarks on a post as the track bends to the left. In less than 100m (320ft) turn right to cross a wet meadow on boardwalks; there are several routes across the meadow, the objective being to reach rough grass and a little hide at the top end.

After the hide, turn right at a white waymark at the end of the meadow, along a wide grass track with several gates and stiles, bearing left across the front of Hall Farm Barn, built in the 1790s and restored about 20 years ago.

Opposite the front of the barn turn sharp right, to walk along a field boundary, with Mannington Hall in view ahead. A stile in 40m (45yds) gives a choice for the next part of the route; go over this and turn right or continue along the edge of the meadow.

On reaching a minor road turn right and then, in 50m (55yds), turn left at an iron gate with waymark. A lovely path now winds through largely coppiced woodland, another important wildlife habitat. Turn right at a clearing, go over a little footbridge and stile and follow the edge of Bridge Meadow, in process of being returned to its original state. As the track bends to the left, ignore a stile on the right.

Opposite a post with many waymarks, turn right into a tunnel through the foliage and along an attractive green lane, rising gently between banks rich in bramble. Go straight on at a junction to reach the edge of Mossymere Wood. (A diversion through the wood along a waymarked path adds to the walk; it is essential to keep bearing right to return to the main route close to a dwelling).

Continue as the track bends to the right to head north. Pass a dwelling on the left, then a part ruinous farm building and continue to join the public road. Turn right to return to the visitor centre in approximately 400m (1280ft).

2 Blakeney and Cley

There are a few parking places by the quay in Blakeney. From the eastern end of the quay walk inland, up High Street. There are two car parks which might be preferred to the quayside parking, particularly at busy periods.

Go straight across the A149 into Wiveton Road, passing the church with its massive tower. Follow the road, between cornfields with bindweed and field-edge poppies adding colour. The Bell Inn is soon reached, facing Wiveton Church across a green. Most of Wiveton village is to the left.

Go straight on, following a 'Cley' signpost downhill to a bridge over the River Glaven.

Turn left at a crossroads with a 'Cley 1' signpost and go along a minor road, to reach a large green with an inn and St Margaret's church, Cley.

Turn right, to rise through the churchyard, then exit by a small gate, turning left along a surfaced lane leading into the main part of Cley, passing the village hall on the right. The road becomes a cul de sac, with a pottery down a track on the left.

Just as further progress seems to be barred, and the road loses its surface, go round to the left. In 20m (70.5ft) follow sign on the right 'to Cley Mill and High Street', go under arch to cross the main road and take the unmade roadway to visit the windmill.

Return to the main road and turn right to pass several shops. Go round a sharp right hand bend at a road junction and then, in 50m (176ft), go up a few steps on the right at a signpost 'Blakeney, 4km (2.5miles), Norfolk Coast Path' The route now follows coastal defence embankments. Cross the river on a footbridge and shortly turn right at a gate/stile towards the sea. The view of Cley Mill from the embankment is very fine.

Turn left at a junction with a 'Protection of Sea Defences' notice. On reaching a wide creek, with shingle beach beyond, turn left to continue along the top of the embankment. Far to the right is the hull of a beached ship, as the path bears to the left to head for Blakeney. Bear left at a junction, pass another wreck and then a small waterfowl reserve to reach Blakeney Quay.

Fine cycling country, like most of East Anglia. 'Marriott's Way', based on Reepham, has already been described above and the 'Norfolk Coast Cycleway' follows quiet roads and lanes through varied countryside between King's Lynn and Cromer. Copies of a detailed map and guide to this designated and marked route are available from Tourist Information Centres in the coastal area. The Norfolk Cycling Map recommended in the introduction has several suggestions for this area and the Wensum Valley cycling routes are very close to the western fringe.

CYCLE HIRE

A1 Taxis
Sheringham.
☎ 01263 822228.

Glaven Marine Cycleline
Glandford.
☎ 01263 741172.

Footloose Guided Cycle Days operate from the car park of the Bure Valley Railway at Aylsham, offering guided tours starting at 10.15am and lasting about half a day, on Sundays, Mondays and Thursdays throughout the season. ☎ 01263 733903.

Getting ready for the ride, Reepham

Blickling Craft Show

Blickling Hall. Mid-April.
☎ 01263 733084

Norfolk Food and Drink Festival

Blickling Park. Early May.
☎ 01263 733084

Cromer Art Week

Mid-to late May. Tourist Information Centre
☎ 01263 512497

Fellbrigg Coast and Country Craft Show

Fellbrigg Hall. Late May.
☎ 01263 837444

Worstead Village Festival

Late July. Tourist Information Office, Aylsham
☎ 01263 733903

Mundesley Festival

Early August. Tourist Information Centre
☎ 01263 721070

Cromer Carnival Week

Mid-to late August. Tourist Information Centre
☎ 01263 512497

Aylsham Show

Blickling Park. Late August.
☎ 01263 733084

Car Tours: Sheringham, Cromer & North-East Norfolk

From north-east Norfolk, practically the whole of East Anglia is within reach for those who enjoy long excursions. Readily to hand are the towns and villages of the north coast, Norwich, Great Yarmouth and the Norfolk Broads.

Hotels

Blakeney

The Blakeney Hotel
☎ 01263 740797
Fax 740795

Erpingham

The Ark, only 3 rooms,
highly recommended
restaurant
☎ 01263 761535

Great Snoring

**The Old Rectory
Country House Hotel**,
over an acre of walled garden
in a very peaceful setting
☎ 01328 820597 Fax 820048

Fakenham

Wensum Lodge Hotel,
very near to town centre
☎ 01328 862100

Wells-next-the-Sea

The Crown Hotel
☎ 01328 710209 Fax 771432

Nr Cromer

**Elderton Lodge Hotel
and Restaurant**,
Thorpe Market
☎ 01263 833547

Blickling

Buckinghamshire Arms,
traditional inn adjacent to
Blickling Hall
☎ 01263 732133

Guest Houses and B&B

Upper Sheringham

Sheringham Park Lodge
☎ 01263 822056

Aylsham

Wheelers Meadow,
Banningham ☎ 01263 73325

The Old Manse,
Burgh Road,
☎ 01263 731283

Lavenders,
Drakes Loke, Buxton
☎ 01603 279179

Nr Cromer

Shrublands Farm,
Northrepps
☎ and Fax 01263 579297

Self-catering

Near Fakenham

Vere Lodge,
South Raynham, 14 cottages
☎ 01328 838362 Fax 838300

The Paddocks,
Little Barney, 3 properties
☎ 01328 878803 and 878802

Caravan and Camping Sites

Fakenham

The Race Course Caravan Site
☎ 01328 862388

Brick Kilns Caravan Site,
Barney (8km (5m) from
Fakenham) ☎ 01328 878305

Cromer

Manor Farm Camping and Caravan Site,
East Runton
☎ 01263 518858

Aylsham

Little Haven Camping and Caravan Park,
Erpingham
☎ 01263 768959

Eating Out

Fakenham

The Old Stable Restaurant,
superb cooking by chef/proprietor
☎ 01328 855947 or 01760 721928

Holt

The Owl Tearooms
☎ 01263 713232

Little Walsingham

The Old Bakehouse Restaurant
☎ 01328 820454

Public Transport

The only remaining railway service is on the 'Bittern Line', connecting Sheringham, Cromer and Norwich, with seven intermediate stops, including North Walsham, Worstead and Wroxham. Trains are at approximately hourly intervals (two hourly on Sundays).

Bus services are more plentiful; the information in Chapter 2 concerning the long distance coastal service and the discounted Day Ranger and Sunday Rover tickets applies equally to the area covered by this chapter. Norfolk Bus Information Centre,
☎ (freecall) 0500 626116.

The showing of a valid bus or rail ticket entitles a discounted admission charge at many of the visitor attractions.

4 NORWICH & THE NORFOLK BROADS

The distinctive Norfolk Broads are probably better known than any other part of East Anglia. Perhaps even more than the Fens, the Broads have come to typify a general impression of the whole area – flat and with a great deal of water. In recent years this unique landscape has been added to the distinguished company of National Parks, giving the extra protection and resources to safeguard its future.

Although the area is always referred to as the 'Norfolk Broads', the southern part is in Suffolk. A small part of the latter county is, therefore, included in this chapter. In terms of 'itinerary' it is appropriate to consider the north – the Rivers Bure Ant and Thurne and their associated broads –

and the south – the Rivers Yare, Waveney and Chet and their associated broads.

Cruising and boating holidays are the dominant attraction of this immensely popular area. But the area also has one of Britain's liveliest seaside resorts in Great Yarmouth and, above all, the

Above: The Cloisters, Norwich Cathedral

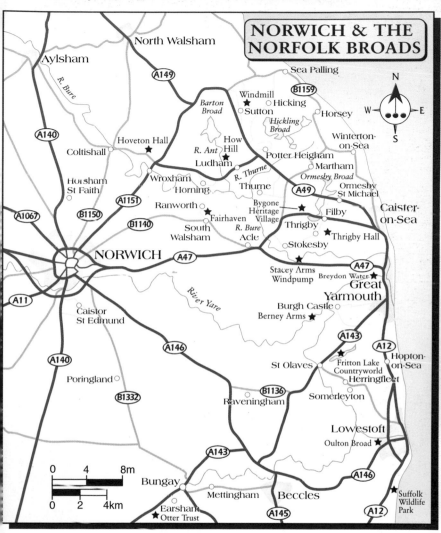

wonderful city of Norwich. The shape of the following itinerary is strongly influenced by the layout of the rivers and the many lakes, both large and small, collectively known as the 'Broads' which in this area have a profound effect on road communications, resulting in some very roundabout routes.

Norwich

A good place to start is at **Norwich**, the 'capital' of East Anglia, said by Nikolaus Pevsner, with only a little exaggeration, to have everything, strategically situated at the hub of a network of major roads and of railway services, at the western end of the Broads holiday area. By city standards Norwich is compact, with the majority of attractive and interesting features within easy walking distance of one another and of car parks, bus and railway stations. For attractions outside the city centre, local bus services are good.

The origins of Norwich go back to well before the Norman Conquest; coins minted early in the 10th century carry the name of the city and, by the time of the Conquest, the city was one of England's largest, with a population of well over 5000. In early times the development of the wool trade increased local prosperity, as did the fertile surrounding countryside. The Rivers Wensum and Yare combined to give a navigable route to the sea at the present Great Yarmouth.

Despite the general material prosperity, the city and its area have, over the centuries, seen more than their fair share of strife. In 1272, disagreement over the levying of tolls on animal fairs by the then dominant monastery resulted in riots and a pitched battle of citizens versus monks.

The Mayor was killed during the Peasants' Revolt in 1381 and 'Kett's Rebellion' against the enclosure of common land in 1549 was very much a Norfolk affair. After the latter rebellion was put down, Robert Kett was hanged from the walls of the castle. In the calmer times of the late 16th century, many skilled weavers arrived from the Netherlands and were involved in the revival of the textile industry.

Today's reminders of the city's history are very fine indeed.

Norwich Cathedral

The **Norman cathedral** is one of England's greatest, started at the end of the 11th century by the first Bishop of Norwich, Herbert de Losinga. The distinctive white stone of the exterior was imported from Caen, in Normandy, ending its water-borne journey along a little canal connecting the cathedral to the nearby river, dug especially for this purpose.

Inside the cathedral, among many fine features, the roof of the nave is of particular interest, with detailed viewing aided by mirrors. A stone effigy, probably of about AD1100,14th century wall paintings by local artists and the cloisters all rank highly in visitor interest. The 96m (315ft) spire, second only to Salisbury in this country, was added at the end of the 15th century.

Close to the south door is the simple grave of Nurse Edith Cavell, shot by the Germans in 1916 for helping the escape of Allied prisoners from occupied Belgium. Running down to the

The extensive collection at the **Castle Museum** includes the art, archaeology and natural history of Norfolk. Paintings focus strongly on the Norfolk School, headed by John Crome and John Cotman, supplemented by a good collection of 17th century Dutch and Flemish work. The museum also has the world's finest collection of Lowestoft porcelain, weapons and musical instruments. There are periodic visiting exhibitions of importance. On the same site are the Regimental Museum of the Royal Norfolk Regiment and the Whistler Theatre.

A notable feature of Norwich is the extensive use made of redundant churches. **St Peter, Hungate**, which has a 15th century hammerbeam roof, houses religious arts and crafts. **St Michael's Church** in Coslany Street has 'Inspire', a 'hands on' science centre with many interesting exhibits and constructions for the young and the not so young.

Quite different is **The Mustard Shop** at 3, Bridewell Alley, where the original shop still trades and there is a small museum at the rear displaying the history of Colman's mustard. Further along the same street, the **Bridewell Museum** occupies a building which was a prison for beggars and tramps.

Dragon Hall in King Street was hidden from view for five centuries. This splendid medieval cloth merchant's hall, with timber framing and a superb crown post roof, has been restored and is open to the public.

Cinema City, the Playhouse and the Maddergate Theatre provide a range of entertainment.

river at Pull's Ferry, the Cathedral Close and Ferry Lane have a wealth of good buildings. The Ferry is long gone; the wharf here served the monastic community at the cathedral and was the start point of the ancient canal.

Norwich Castle

Almost as old as the cathedral, the construction of the great **Norman castle** was started early in the 12th century, with the walls again being of Caen stone, refaced with Bath stone in 1834-39. The huge keep now looks rather less than warlike in its use as a museum. Additional defences for the city were provided in the 14th century, when 6m (20ft) walls were erected, with 10 fortified gateways and a series of towers, now best seen at Carrow Hill, where a section of wall climbs to Black Tower.

Other survivors from early times include **Strangers Hall** (early 14th century) and the finely carved **Erpingham Gate** of 1420, opposite the cathedral west front, donated by Sir Thomas Erpingham who commanded the archers at the battle of Agincourt and features in Shakespeare's 'King Henry V'.

Beside the cathedral is King Edward VI School and a statue of the most famous pupil, Horatio (later Lord) Nelson, whose education certainly seems to have been spread around Norfolk.

Modern Norwich

Modern Norwich is closely integrated into the ancient framework. Indeed the recent Castle Mall shopping centre, with entrances close to the Market Square, is brilliantly incorporated into the mound beside the castle, with its elegant glass and iron roof forming part of the 4 acres of public space, mainly grass, water features and promenades, enhanced by the partially outdoor cafes of the shopping centre.

Norwich was a pioneer of city centre pedestrianisation, which now contributes a great deal to the enjoyment of wandering along the narrow old streets, where speciality shops and restaurants complement the city's major department stores.

The huge **market place** is central, sitting below the City Hall, opened by King George VI in 1938. To one side is the early 15th century **Guildhall**, now housing the **Tourist Information Centre**. To the other side is St Peter Mancroft, with perpendicular architecture, one of the finest of the city's many churches.

Towards the edge of the city centre, quite close to the cathedral, the short, hilly, little street known as Elm Hill has a wonderful old world atmosphere, cobble-paved street and timber framed colour washed buildings, housing galleries, antique shops and a pottery.

Outside the city centre are two further attractions of note. At the University of East Anglia, the **Sainsbury Centre for Visual Arts** is a modern gallery in an ultra modern building which visitors either love or hate. Here, the collection of Robert and Lisa Sainsbury includes a great deal of modern western art and fine arts from all over the world. Featuring strongly are Francis Bacon, Henry Moore and Alberto Giacometti.

On a more modest scale, is the City of Norwich **Aviation Museum** at Old Norwich Road, Horsham St Faith. Aircraft, engines, memorabilia and an exhibition of the local role of the US Air Force are on display in a constantly improving collection.

Public parks and open spaces feature strongly in Norwich, with a June and July season of free open-air theatre at five venues. The river also plays its part, with a popular riverside footpath. River cruises include the River Wensum and part of the Broads and there is a river bus from Elm Hill to Thorpe Station.

A 'Park and Ride' system with four centres outside the city (Harford, Hewett, Airport, Postwick) is a great asset for visitors preferring to leave their vehicles outside the busy centre.

Daytime general guided walking tours of about 1 hour's duration are available from April to October. Evening tours based around special themes operate from May to August. All start at the Guildhall.

• Coleman's Mustard •

Mustard has been grown in England since Roman times. In the early years of the 19th century Jeremiah Coleman founded what was to become the largest mustard manufaturing company and an English household name. Coleman's distinctive yellow tins are familiar to generations.

The mustard seeds were crushed to make a fine powder. Everything was made on site at Carrow Mills in Norwich, including the wooden casks and printed labels. The story of Colemans is told in the museum behind the attractive Mustard Shop.

Coleman's Mustard shop, Norwich

Norwich Castle Museum

Rotunda coffee shop, provision for disabled visitors, including wheelchair and lift. Open daily, Monday to Saturday, 10.00 to 17.00. Sunday, 14.00 to 17.00.
☎ 01603 493624.

Inspire

St Michael's Church, Coslany Street. Gift shop and basic refreshments. Open from Tuesday to Sunday, 10.00 to 17.30 (last admission 16.30).
☎ 01603 612612.

Dragon Hall

115-121, King Street. Medieval cloth merchants' hall. Mostly accessible to people with disabilities. Open April to October, Monday to Saturday, 10.00 to 16.00. November to March, Monday to Friday, 10.00 to 16.00. Closed from just before Christmas to the beginning of January and on Bank Holidays.
☎ 01603 663922.

The Mustard Shop

3, Bridewell Alley. Open during usual shop hours.

Sainsbury Centre for Visual Arts

University of East Anglia. Coffee bar. Facilities for the disabled, including electric wheelchair. Open from Tuesday to Sunday, 11.00 to 17.00.
☎ 01603 456060.

City of Norwich Aviation Museum

Horsham St Faith. Souvenir shop and tearoom. Open beginning of April to the end of October, daily except Wednesday, 10.00 to 17.00, plus 19.30 to dusk and Wednesday afternoons from May to August. From the beginning of November to the end of March, Wednesday, Saturday and Sunday, 10.00 to 16.00. Closed from just before Christmas to early in the New Year.
☎ 01603 625309.

Theatre in the Parks

June and July evenings.
☎ 01603 212137.

River and Broads Cruises

Southern River Steamers
☎ 01603 624051.

Guided Walking Tours

Start at the Guildhall
☎ 01603 666071.

Wroxham to Stalham

A few miles to the north-east of Norwich, the small town of Wroxham is quite a holiday centre by the side of the River Bure, its popularity very much centred on pleasure boating, with abundant boatyards and moorings.

Roy's of Wroxham is world famous as the 'biggest village store in Britain', an emporium occupying several buildings in Wroxham, with some branches elsewhere. Always busy in season, Wroxham also has the southern terminus of the Bure Valley Railway, a narrow gauge, largely steam hauled, line (see Aylsham in Chapter 3).

The village is a starting point for a variety of river and broad tours on large launches, and small craft, for day and part day hire. The adjacent village of **Hoveton** shares a common boundary at the bridge over the River Bure; many of the facilities are, in fact, in Hoveton but this need not concern the visitor. The name 'Wroxham' can serve for both.

There is a railway station on the 'Bittern' line which connects Sheringham, Cromer and Norwich. A short diversion to the west leads to **Coltishall**, a large village on the River Bure. It is notable as the head of navigation for pleasure cruisers on that river. There is a strong World War II RAF and US air force history in this area, as in so much of East Anglia. Coltishall has a station on the Bure Valley Railway. To the south, along the B1150, at Redwings Horse Sanctuary, badly treated horses, ponies, donkeys and mules are given a new lease of life.

Five kilometres (3 miles) north of Wroxham, **Wroxham Barns** is a major rural craft centre, with many kinds of workshop, gift shops and tearooms, augmented by Williamson's Traditional Family Fair and a junior farm. Close by, **Hoveton Hall Gardens** and tearooms offer a very fine garden, rich in rhododendrons and hydrangeas, with an attractive lake.

In the same vicinity, **Willow Farm Flowers Dried Flower Centre** is a more unusual attraction. This is a family farm with thatched barn and several acres of growing flowers, all to be dried. Flower arranging demonstrations are given and there are guided farm walks.

Horning is a substantial village along the side of the River Bure below Wroxham. The street hugging close to the river is quite pretty and is well defined by an inn at each end. The Ferry Inn is a Broads focal point, with plentiful moorings, obviously popular with the boating fraternity.

Continuing away from Wroxham, next is **Ludham Bridge**, with moorings, shop and cafe. **Ludham** village is well provided with shops, inn, restaurant and tearoom.

Continued on page 96...

93

Two thousand or so years ago there was a vast and complex estuary with its mouth between present day Caister-on-Sea and the high ground at Burgh Castle, extending inland for several miles up what are now the Rivers Bure, Ant, Yare and Waveney. The formation of a shingle spit partially blocked the mouth of this estuary, forcing the waters of the Rivers Yare and Bure to divert to the south. Progressive silting followed and, by the time of the Norman conquest, the fishing community of Yarmouth was established on the spit.

The Broads is often thought of as a fine 'natural' landscape; however, like the great majority of English landscapes, this is far from the truth. Twentieth century research has revealed that extensive peat digging in medieval times created huge but shallow hollows into which water seeped, creating the numerous lakes large and small now collectively known as the Broads.

The study of monastic records has helped in this discovery; in the early 14th century Norwich Cathedral Priory purchased something like 400,000 turves as fuel. The rising water levels inevitably killed off the digging process.

The succeeding centuries saw the development of a distinct way of life among the lakes, the dykes and the huge beds of sedge and reed. Fishing, eel and duck catching and the cutting of the reed and the sedge provided work and a living for the sparse population.

The need to produce food from the land to supplement that obtained from nature led to a great deal of drainage of the marshes by systems of dykes and windpumps, many of which remain as a highly characteristic feature of the Broads landscape. In this way, grazing marshes were created.

In modern times traditional industries faded as the build up of sewage wastes, agricultural chemicals and pollution of all types from the intensive use by pleasure boats has

The Staithe, Luddham

affected water quality and reduced the richness and diversity of plant and animal life. Open water is now much less and the gradual conversion of the edges to fen, then carr (largely alder), then oak woodland, is proceeding steadily.

Some years ago a start was made in attempting to maintain areas of the unique wetland habitat by improving water quality to allow the return of the original vegetation and the associated wildlife. **Cockshoot Broad** is an example of what can be achieved.

Perhaps the most important factor in protecting this unique environment is the designation of the area as a National Park in 1989, bringing stronger planning controls and better targeting of resources.

Close by, **Womack Water**, with boatyard and moorings, connects with the River Thurne. St Catherine's Church is 15th century, with 14th century chancel. Inside are a hammerbeam roof, quaint carving on the chancel arch, a screen of 1493 with paintings of saints and a striking well-carved 15th century font. Occupying a lonely site by the side of the River Thurne, the ruins of **St Benet's Abbey**, with the odd superimposition of the tower of a windmill, can be reached from Ludham. A better approach to the Abbey is by river.

Minor roads going north-west from Ludham lead to **How Hill**. Here, the house is used as a residential Broads Study Centre. Apart from the gardens, the adjacent land is open to the public with plenty of space for picnics. **Toad Hole Cottage**, down by the River Ant, has been refurbished as a 19th century eel catcher's cottage. From the adjacent landing stage the 'Electric Eel' an 8 seater boat, operates 50 minute trips, gliding almost silently along the dykes among the traditional reed beds, with excellent viewing of the abundant wildlife.

From Horning a minor road heads up the west side of **Barton Broad**, weaving in and out to visit tiny villages and hamlets, such as Irstead, Nettishead, with inn, and Barton Turf, after which the main A1151 road must be joined, turning right to Wayford Bridge and on to Stalham. There are two nature reserves on this side of the Broad.

Situated at the northern extremity of the Broads, **Stalham** is one of the smaller, quieter Norfolk towns, with a small market each Tuesday. The one long street has inns and restaurants and a fair range of individual shops, bounded by the church at one end and the post office at the other. Boats reach the town by a channel at the north end of Barton Broad; there are staithes ('staithe' means landing place, quay) and a small boat building industry.

Museum of the Broads – see page 100.

Sutton to Ranworth

Sutton and its well known **windmill** are a short distance to the south from Stalham. The mill is claimed to be the tallest in Britain, with nine floors and a viewing gallery. Much milling machinery is still in situ and the mill is subject to a long term renovation programme. It remained in use until 1940.

Adjacent to the mill is a comprehensive and fascinating personal collection of bygones, with excellent reconstructions, notably of a pharmacy. This was installed in Shanklin, Isle of Wight, in the 1880s and was brought to Sutton in 1991. Other exhibits include a tobacco shop, engines and trade tricycles. Close by, in Church Road, is the small but interesting **Sutton Pottery**,

Bure Valley Railway

See Aylsham in Chapter 3.

Wroxham Barns

Rural craft centre. Tearooms, shops, facilities for the disabled. Open every day except Christmas Day and Boxing Day, 10.00 to 17.00. Fair is open Easter to early September, 11.00 to 17.00.
☎ 01603 783762.

Hoveton Hall Gardens

North of Wroxham, 5km (3 miles). Old Milking Parlour tearoom. Open from Easter Sunday to mid-September, Wednesday, Friday, Sunday and Bank Holiday Mondays, 11.00 to 17.30.
☎ 01603 782798.

Redwings Horse Sanctuary

Frettenham, Norwich. Open Sundays and Bank Holidays from Easter to early December and Mondays during July and August, 12.30 to 17.00.
☎ 01603 737432.

Willow Farm Flowers Dried Flower Centre

Near Hoveton, north of Wroxham. Picnic and play area, drinks and ice creams.

Open from Tuesday to Saturday, 10.00 to 16.00, Sunday 11.00 to 16.00, Bank Holidays, 10.00 to 16.00.

Toad Hall Cottage

How Hill, Ludham. Refurbished eel catcher's cottage. Boat excursions and walking trails. Information; maps and souvenirs for sale. Open Easter to May and October, weekends, Bank Holidays and local half-term, 11.00 to 15.00. June to September, daily, 10.00 to 17.00.
☎ 01692 678763.

Cruises and Boat Hire

Broads Tours

Wroxham and Potter Heigham. Cruises and day boat hire. May to August.
☎ O1603 782207.

George Smith and Sons

Wroxham. Day boat hire; cruises with facilities for the disabled. Open all year.
☎ 01603 782527.

Museum of the Broads

Stalham Staithe.
Open daily April to September, 11.00 to 1700.
☎ 01692 581681

where work in progress can be watched.

From Sutton, minor roads lead across country to **Hickling**. At the north end of the Broad, The Pleasure Boat Inn at Hickling Heath has moorings and 2 hour Broad exploration trips in a small boat.

Three kilometres (2 miles) further, with some care in the route finding, is the **Hickling Broad Nature Reserve Visitor Centre**, operated by the Norfolk Wildlife Trust. Colour waymarked trails, some with boardwalks, wind through reed beds and marshes

Above: The Wildlife Gardens, Thrigby Hall
Below: The dried flower centre, near Wroxham

beside the Broad, among a wealth of wildlife. The Visitor Centre has the usual information, gift shop, hot and cold drinks and ice cream.

Most of this part of the Norfolk coast consists of a long line of sea defences backing a sandy beach, without significant features. **Sea Palling** lies just inland, with an inn; at the nearby sea front another inn is accompanied by a few shops of post-war construction, with water sports on the award winning beach.

The coast road (B1159) continues to **Horsey** and **Horsey Mill**, the latter owned by the National Trust, with car park, public conveniences and the small Staithe Stores where hot and cold drinks and ice cream may be purchased. The former drainage mill of 1912 was struck by lightening in 1943 and put out of action. The tower is noted for its view and there is surviving machinery.

To return to the coast from Sutton, head for **Winterton-on-Sea**, where the church tower is visible well out to sea, and the beach is backed by inn, car park and public conveniences. Continuing to the south, Hemsby, Newport, Scratby and California all have extensive holiday park type visitor accommodation, with appropriate, shops, catering and amusements.

Caister-on-Sea is a much larger, mainly modern, residential town with a small shopping centre, separated from Great Yarmouth by the race course and not much else. The name 'Caister' indicates the town origins as a Roman camp. Helped by the brown road signs, the site of the camp is not difficult to find; the key is the roundabout where the B1159 joins A149 on the inland edge of the town.

Just inland from Caister, the A1064 leads to the well-signposted privately owned **Caister Castle Car Collection**, with more than 200 exhibits housed in a purpose-built large exhibition centre in the grounds attached to the ruins of the medieval Caister Castle.

The main road to Rollesby, by-passing Ormesby St Margaret, soon reaches **Norfolk Rare Breeds Centre** at Decoy Farm House, Ormesby St Michael, where rare breeds of cattle, sheep, pigs and other farm and domestic animals are on display.

Martham is a large village, pleasant enough, with some Georgian houses in the middle, but not of particular visitor interest. For those who like to seek out quiet backwaters, there is a lane to the north leading in 1km (0.5 mile) to the River Thurne at Martham Ferry (no operational ferry), with moorings along Martham Staithe.

Potter Heigham is a key centre in the northern part of the Broads, with extensive boatyards and all boating facilities. The road bridge over the River Thurne has long been notorious as a test of steely nerves for amateur helmsmen steering a large cruiser through with literally inches to spare, whilst top deck sunbathers leap for safety.

Potter Heigham divides naturally into three communities: the boating area by the bridge, with shops and cafes aimed at visitors; the small old village 1km (0.5 mile) to the north-west; and a detached residential area on the north-east side of the A149.

The **Museum of the Broads** has recently (1999) moved to Stalham, see page 97. Displays of Broads history, traditional industries and local curiosities are supplemented by video and slide shows. The collection is growing and the policy is one of continuous expansion aimed at creating a major museum, with 'Man's Effect on the Broadland Environment' as the theme.

Heading back in a southerly direction, a turn to the west reaches **Thurne** hamlet in an isolated position by the side of the River Bure, with inn, moorings and a well known windmill. Back to the east, through **Burgh St Margaret (Fleggburgh)**.

The **Bygone Village** is spaciously laid out with a wide range of attractions including a short railway line, vintage vehicles, motor cycles, traditional fairground, concert hall, with reconstructions such as forge and village school. Live shows including puppets. Shops, catering, woodland walks and parkland picnics.

A lane to the south from **Filby** leads to **Thrigby Hall Wildlife Gardens** where a well-presented collection of Asian animals and birds occupies the grounds of the Hall, an attractive old building. With just a few exceptions, the title 'Zoo' is now avoided for animal premises, presumably on grounds of political correctness! Tigers, monkeys, crocodiles, alligators and storks are all well represented. There is a children's play area and the usual visitor facilities.

Returning to the main B1152, the River Bure is crossed at **Acle Bridge** (moorings and inn) to reach the area to the south of the river and of the series of Broads which block road communication between this area and Horning/Ludham. **Acle** is a small town with a fair range of shops and a market on Thursdays. There are moorings at Acle Dyke, connecting to the River Bure. **The Stracey Arms windpump**, with the inn adjacent, is nearly 5km (3 miles) downstream. **Stokesby**, on the north bank of the river, is a pleasant riverside village, with green and moorings.

North-west of Acle, close to the modest village of South Walsham, **Fairhaven Woodland and Water Gardens**, of 170 acres, were developed in 1947 by Lord Fairhaven into an attractive area, retaining the original dykes by the edge of South Walsham Broad.

Pleasure Boating on the Norfolk Broads

Approximately 200km (125 miles) of lock-free navigation on the rivers, cuts and associated Broads has huge appeal for thousands of boat owners, ranging from small dinghies to well-equipped large pleasure cruisers and sailing boats. Even more thousands of visitors and holiday makers hire a boat by the hour, the day or the week, to don their nautical caps and cruise happily through these waterways. Many of the attractions such as drainage mills and waterside inns are more readily accessible by boat.

On-shore facilities for boat users are widely available and the more important centres such as Norwich, Wroxham, Great Yarmouth, Potter Heigham, Oulton Broad and Beccles have fuel, waste disposal, shower and toilet blocks adjacent to the extensive moorings. Despite the abundance of moorings, crowding does occur in high season.

For ecological and safety reasons, there are strict rules laid down and enforced by the Broads Authority. In particular, the speed limits, ranging from 3-6mph (5-10kmph) must always be observed.

A list of some of the principal boat hirers is included in the FactFile.

The gardens are seen at their best in Spring and early Summer.

Ranworth Broad is banned to pleasure boats and is now of national and international importance for wildlife, forming part of the large **Bure Marshes National Nature Reserve**. A nature trail leads through woodland and reed beds (boardwalk) to the floating conservation centre, well equipped and with extensive views over the open water (binoculars provided). Common tern, great crested grebes and, in winter, teal, widgeon, shoveller, pochard and gadwall come here to feed. The Broad is also an inland roost for cormorants.

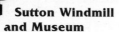

Sutton Windmill and Museum

Gift shop. Open from the beginning of April to the end of September, daily, 10.00 to 17.30.
☎ 01692 581195.

Sutton Pottery

Opening hours not publicised.
☎ 01692 580595.

Horsey Mill

National Trust Windpump. General stores with hot and cold drinks and ice cream. Open from late March to the end of September, daily, 11.00 to 17.00.
☎ 01493 393904.

Hickling Broad Nature Reserve Visitor Centre

Shop, refreshments and toilets. Disabled access along the boardwalk and trail to the Broad. Open all year, daily, 10.00 to 17.00.
☎ 01692 598276.

Roman Fort

Caister. Open at all reasonable hours.

Caister Castle Car Collection

Light refreshments, picnic area and disabled facilities. Open from the last week in May to the last Friday in September, daily except Saturdays, 10.00 to 16.30.
☎ 01572 787251.

Norfolk Rare Breeds Centre

Decoy House Farm, Ormesby St Michael. Open from early January to late March, Sunday 11.00 to 16.00. Late March to the end of October, daily except Saturday, 11.00 to 17.00. November and December, Sunday, 11.00 to 16.00.
☎ 01493 732990.

Broads Tours

Potter Heigham. River trips and day boats. May to August. ☎ 01692 670711.

Bygone Village

Burgh St Margaret (Fleggburgh). Restaurant and other catering. Extensive visitor facilities. Open from early April to the beginning of November, 10.00 to 17.00 (many attractions closed on Saturdays). Telephone for winter opening details.
☎ 0990 134890.

Thrigby Hall Wildlife Gardens

Cafe. Open every day of the year, 10.00 to 17.30.
☎ 01493 369477.

The Candlemaker

Stokesby. Open from March to October, from 09.00 daily. Winter opening, times may vary.
☎ 01493 750242.

Fairhaven Woodland and Water Gardens

South Walsham. Restaurant, plant sales and gift shop. Open from Good Friday to the beginning of October, daily except Monday (open on Bank Holiday Mondays) 11.00 to 17.30.
☎ 01603 270449.

Bure Marshes National Nature Reserve

Ranworth Broad. Visitor Centre, conservation centre. Hot and cold drinks and ice cream. Open (visitor centre) from April to October, daily, 10.00 to 17.00.
☎ 01603 270479.

Displays of former kitchen products, Sutton Mill Museum

Great Yarmouth

Gateway to the southern Broads. A shorter itinerary starts at Great Yarmouth, which can be regarded as three places in one. Firstly, a port facing inland across the River Yare, backed by the unlovely industrial and commercial area of the Denes. Secondly a sizeable market town with a good shopping centre and large residential suburbs, and thirdly a major holiday and visitor resort with a long Marine Parade behind a sandy beach, two piers and the usual range of seaside attractions.

The town is sited on a spit of land between the Yare and the North Sea, formed many centuries ago by progressive silting. The Romans had a presence at neighbouring Caister-on-Sea, but in Great Yarmouth it is medieval remains which are apparent.

Sections of the old town wall are best seen at the **North West Tower** of 1344. This stands close to the river, a little way beyond the most northerly of the road bridges across the river, and a short distance behind St Nicholas Church. The Tower is now a small museum.

South of the Market Place and behind South Quay was an area of congested courts and alleys called **The Rows**, 145 in all, set out in a grid pattern which still defines the shape of this part of the town, although damage during World War II was considerable. On South Quay itself, a row of Tudor, Georgian and Victorian buildings combine to form a fine inland-facing waterfront.

In this area is **The Elizabethan House**, 4 South Quay, a 16th century merchant's house, now a museum of domestic life. Close by are the **Row 111** house and the **Old Merchant's House**, owned by English Heritage and operated as a joint attraction, contrasting the housing of the richer and the poorer classes in this area. There are good plaster ceilings and an exhibition of historic local architectural fittings. Entrance is by guided tour only. The 13th century **Greyfriars Cloisters**, with some early wall paintings is part of the same visitor complex.

In nearby Tollhouse Street the late 13th century **Tollhouse** is said to be the oldest civic building in Britain. The dungeons are open to the public, as is a local history museum and brass rubbing centre. The 'Lydia Eve', last of the once numerous steam drifter fishing boats, is periodically moored at South Quay as a visitor attraction.

More modern Great Yarmouth is centred on the vast Market Place (markets on Wednesday, Saturday and summer Fridays), with a shopping area including an elegant arcade. The large 12th century parish church of St Nicholas, restored after a World War II fire, is at the north end. Adjacent, in a timber-framed cottage is the birthplace of Anna Sewell, author of the well loved children's book **'Black Beauty'**.

At the north-east corner of the Market Place is the group of almshouses called the **Fishermen's Hospice,** restored and improved in 1985-86, for 'decayed fishermen'. The draconian rules governing the behaviour of the residents are set out on a wall-board.

On the sea front is the **Great Yarmouth Maritime Museum,** displaying the story of the local coast. Perhaps unexpectedly, there is yet another Nelson link. He stands isolated on a column soaring above the mediocre surroundings of the Denes area on which he is condemned to gaze in perpetuity.

The holiday resort really needs little further description as it does its best to emulate Blackpool. Theatres, sports and leisure centre, race courses for horses and greyhounds, pleasure beach, sea life centre, stock car racing and amusement arcades all compete to entertain the visitor.

The town has railway services to Norwich and beyond, with a choice of route through the Broads countryside.

Places to Visit: *Great Yarmouth*

North West Tower

North Quay. Open from July to September, daily 10.00 to 16.00.
☎ 01493 332095.

Elizabethan House

4, South Quay (National Trust). Open early April to mid-April, daily except Saturday, 10.00 to 17.00 (opens at 14.00 on Sundays). Late May to late September, daily except Saturday, 10.00 to 17.00.
☎ 01493 855 746.

Old Merchant's House/ Row 111 House/ Greyfriars Cloisters

Open from the beginning of April to the beginning of November, daily, 10.00 to 17.00 (closed 13.00 to 14.00) for guided tours only, departing on the hour (up to 16.00) from the Row 111 house.
☎ 01493 857900.

Maritime Museum

Marine Parade. Open during Easter and early holidays, Monday to Friday 10.00 to 17.00, Sunday 14.00 to 17.00. Late May to late September, daily except Saturday, 10.00 to 17.00.
☎ 01493 842267.

Burgh Castle to Bungay

The area immediately inland from Great Yarmouth is rich in visitor interest. **Burgh Castle** is the site of the Roman fort Gariannonum, situated on a mound which towers over the flat marshes by the head of Breydon Water, with the **Berney Arms Mill**, a noted Broadland landmark, clearly in view.

From the car park at the entrance to Church Farm, the fort is less than 1km (0.5 mile) on foot. A Norman motte and bailey castle was superimposed on the Roman site; strong stone walls, up to about 5 metres (16ft) in height survive on three sides of the rectangle, the fourth side having slid down the steep western slope. There is a burial ground to the east of the fort.

Fritton parish church has a round tower with a Norman base and a 15th century top. The nave roof is thatched. Inside is a restored early 16th century oak screen with old paintings, carved font and three decker pulpit. **Fritton Lake Countryworld** has a large lake with rowing boats, 9 hole golf course, putting, railway, craft centre, pony rides, waterfowl, falconry displays, children's farmyard and adventure playground.

Somerleyton Hall and twelve acres of garden feature a famous maze, established in yew in 1846, good statuary and the Loggia Tearooms. An early Victorian mansion, the Hall is the home of Lord and Lady Somerleyton. There is a strong Italian influence in the design, with a great deal of carved stone. Some state rooms are very fine, with pictures by Landseer and Wright of Derby. Wood carving by Grinling Gibbons and glasshouses by Paxton are also featured.

Herringfleet Smock Mill, dating from the 1830s, was the last operational mill of its type. It stands beside the River Waveney and can be reached by an easy footpath, mainly across grazing marshes, but with several gates and stiles to negotiate. The distance is less than 1km (0.5 mile). The footpath is signposted by the side of the B1074, less than 1km (0.5 mile) north-west of Herringfleet church. There is a small parking layby adjacent.

The ruins of **St Olave's** Priory are a short distance along a rough track to the right, approximately 150m (160yds) on the Yarmouth side of the road bridge across the River Waveney. There is a good deal of rare medieval brickwork including a notable refectory undercroft with brick fan vaulting dating from about 1300. After the Dissolution of the Monasteries only a Prior and five Canons remained. If the undercroft door is locked, the key is obtainable from Priory House nearby.

Once having crossed the River Waveney at St Olave's, visitor attractions are rather more thin on the ground. The A143 leads towards **Beccles**, a busy Suffolk market town, very much part of the Broadland scene. Following major fires in the 16th and 17th centuries, Beccles is now a mellow town of red brick Georgian houses, many showing Dutch influence. The 30m (97ft) tall bell tower of the parish church of St Michael stands apart from the main building.

Also of interest are the 18th century **octagonal town hall** and the **Town Museum** in Ballygate. The latter occupies a beautiful building and exhibits concentrate on showing social aspects of life in the town. On Newgate, William Clowes have operated a printing business since 1870. The comprehensive **Printing Museum** was established in 1984 to commemorate the 400th anniversary of the granting of the town's charter.

The Quay is an important boating centre quite close to the head of navigation on the River Waveney, at Geldeston lock, about 4.5km (3 miles) further up river. The Quay has an inn, information centre, public conveniences and children's play area all close to the extensive boat moorings. Beccles railway station has services on the line connecting Ipswich and Lowestoft

Above: Bigod's Castle, Bungay
Below: St Olave's Priory

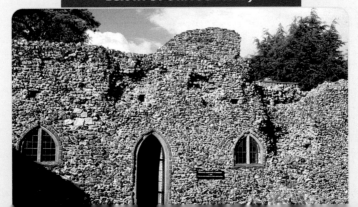

Burgh Castle and Church Farm

Tearoom at farm (Easter to October). Castle open at any reasonable time.

Fritton Lake Countryworld

Cafe and shop. Open every day from early April to late September, 10.00 to 17.30. ☎ 01493 488208.

Somerleyton Hall and Gardens

Tearooms, picnic area. Open from Easter Sunday to the end of Sept, Thurs, Sun and Bank Holidays. Also Tues and Wed in July and August, Hall 13.30 to 17.00, Gardens, 12.30 to 17.30, Tearoom, 12.30 to 17.00.
☎ 01502 730224.

Herringfleet Smock Mill

Open only on occasional days throughout the year, weather permitting, 13.00 to 17.00.
☎ 01473 583352.

St Olave's Priory

English Heritage.
Open at any reasonable time.
☎ 01493 488609.

Raveningham Gardens

Open from early May to late July, Sundays and Bank Holiday Mondays, 14.00 to 17.30. ☎ 01508 548480.

Berney Arms Windmill

English Heritage. Open from beginning of April to begin-ning of November, daily, 09.00 to 17.00 (closed from 13.00 to 14.00).
☎ 01493 700605.

Beccles and District Museum

Open from the beginning of April to the end of October, Tuesday to Sunday and Bank Holiday Mondays, 14.30 to 17.00. ☎ 01502 715722.

Printing Museum

William Clowes Ltd., Newgate, Beccles. Open from June to August, Monday to Friday, 14.00 to 16.30.
☎ 01502 712884.

Winter Flora

Hall Farm, Weston, Beccles. Sale of artificial flowers and garden accessories. Coffee shop. Open daily, 10.00 to 17.00, Sundays, 10.00 to 16.00. Closed Easter Sunday and 24th to 29th December.
☎ 01502 716810.

Station 146 Control Tower

Seething Airfield, near Poringland, off the B1332, Norwich to Bungay road. Refreshments. Open from May to October, first Sunday each month, 10.00 to 17.00.
☎ 01508 550288.

Bigod's Castle

Bungay. Open from Monday to Saturday, 09.00 to 17.00,

Although a little way above
the limit of Broadland boating, it
is logical to include **Bungay** in
this chapter. A compact market
town, clustering tightly around its
market place, with a butter cross
dating from 1689, Bungay has a
fair array of shops, with antiques
well represented. A disastrous
fire in 1688 ensures that most of
the older property is of the 18th
century.

Bigod Castle was built in 1165
and extended in 1294 by members of the family of the same
name, powerful Suffolk landowners of the time. By the late 14th
century it had already become
ruinous. Gate house, bridge pit
and curtain walling remain on
site. Other small remnants may be
found in the town. The small
Bungay Museum is situated in
the council offices in Broad
Street. Two rooms are used to
display coins and miscellaneous
local relics.

At nearby Earsham, the **Otter
Trust** has a large collection of
British and Asian otters in a series of spacious paddocks with
good viewing facilities. Three
lakes with waterfowl, Muntjac
deer, fallow deer and wallabies
add to the interest.

A few kilometres to the north-
east, **Raveningham** has extensive
gardens surrounding the elegant
Georgian house, providing the
setting for many rare and unusual
plants, with sculptures, parkland
and church.

Further to the west, Loddon
and Chedgrave are substantial
villages on either side of the River
Chet, whilst **Reedham** is an important communication point,
with a well-known chain ferry
across the River Yare and a railway junction. The well-preserved,
large but lonely mill at **Berney
Arms** can be reached by train to
the halt about 10 minutes walk
away, or by boat. The mill is the
tallest (seven floors) remaining
marsh mill in working order.

Station 146 Control Tower at
Seething Airfield is south-east
of Poringland, off the B1332,
Norwich to Bungay road. The
restored control tower has relics
of the US Air Force 448th bomb
group which operated with Lib-
erator aircaft from this airfield
during World War II.

Walks: Norwich & the Norfolk Broads

The Broads area is well provided with short walks based on nature trails. A good example is at Hickling Broad, where a 1.5km (1 mile) trail from the visitor centre to the edge of the Broad is partly on boardwalk, partly on gravel and partly on grass, traversing an area rich in wildlife.

The **'Norfolk Walks'** package mentioned in Chapter 2 has routes based on the towns and villages of Stalham, Winterton-on-Sea, Filby, Bradwell, Blofield and Brundall, Great and Little Plumstead, Rackheath and Salhouse. Ten kilometres (6 miles) is the maximum distance; several are much shorter.

The **Weavers' Way** winds through the area of the Broads from Great Yarmouth to North Walsham before heading west to Aylsham and then north to join the Norfolk Coast Path near Cromer.

At Bungay, the **Bigod Way**, a 16km (10 mile) loop encircles the town with connections like the spokes of a wheel providing several walks of varying length. See the information board at the castle, or obtain a leaflet at the Tourist Information Centre

Car Tours: Norwich & the Norfolk Broads

On a fine day the North Norfolk coast (see Chapters 2 and 3) beckons, with Hunstanton, Blakeney, Wells, Sheringham and Cromer all well within reach from any base in this area.

For a different coastal experience, the comparatively undeveloped Suffolk coast to the south can be visited. On this coast, the vanished town of Dunwich and the attractive little towns of Southwold and Aldeburgh **(see Chapter 6)** make fine excursions of a modest distance. For those more technologically minded, the Sizewell nuclear power station has a visitor centre and guided tours of parts of the plant.

Inland Suffolk is noted for its small towns and villages, often dominated by large and beautiful churches, typified by Lavenham and Long Melford. Bury St Edmunds, with cathedral, abbey ruins and much more to see, is the largest town and a focal point **(see Chapter 7)**.

Cycle Rides: Norwich & the Norfolk Broads

Flat country, with numerous attractive destinations and a fair number of quiet lanes adds up to a good place for cyclists. Inevitably, waterways make many of the routes roundabout but, for touring by cycle, arguably this is a plus rather than a minus. A good example is a circuit of 53km (33 miles) from Horning, visiting Ludham, Catfield, Hickling Green, Sutton Mill, East Ruston, Dilham, returning via the west side of Barton Broad, through Barton Turf and Neatishead to Horning.

CYCLE HIRE

Lawford
Great Yarmouth.
☎ 01493 842741.

Just Pedalling
Coltishall.
☎ 01603 737201.

Broads Bike Hire
☎ 01603 782281.

Acle Bridge
☎ 01493 750355.

Ludham Bridge
☎ 01692 630486.

Reedham Quay
☎ 01493 700346.

Sutton Staithe
☎ 01692 581653.

Thurne Staithe
Hoveton.
☎ 01603 783096.

Norfolk Cycling Holidays offer a complete holiday package including accommodation, maps and pre-planned routes for most of the county.
☎ 01485 540642.

Windmill Ways Walking and Cycling Holidays allow you to walk or cycle without luggage.
☎ 01603 871111.

Modern sculpture at the Sainsbury Centre, Norwich University

Hotels

Norwich

The Posthouse
Ipswich Road ☎ 01603
456431 Fax 01602 506400

Dunston Hall Hotel
4m (6kkm) from Norwich,
luxury hotel in 110 acres, 72
rooms
☎ 01508 470444 Fax 471499

Park Farm Country Hotel
Hethersett 38 rooms set in
landscaped gardens
☎ 01603 810264 Fax 812104

The Beeches
Earlham Road
☎ 01603 621167

Guest Houses and B&B

Nr Bungay

Earsham Park Farm
☎ 01986 892180

Nr Norwich

Greenacres Farm
Wood Green, Long Stratton
☎ 01508 530261

Horning

Petersfield House
Lower Street 18 rooms
☎ 01692 630741 Fax 630745

Great Yarmouth

Spindrift Private Hotel
Wellesley Road
☎ and Fax 01493 858674

The Old Court House
Rollesby
☎ 01493 369665

Self-catering

Nr Great Yarmouth

Clippesby Holidays
22 cottages
☎ 01493 369367 Fax 368181

Norwich

Norwich Breaks
5 cottages
☎ 01603 453363 Fax 259729

Spixworth Hall Cottages
4 properties
☎ 01603 898190 Fax 897176

University of East Anglia
17 properties
☎ 01603 593271 Fax 250585

Horning

Premier Marina Cottages
21 properties
☎ 01692 630392
Fax 01692 631040

Overstrand

Poppyland Holiday Cottages
6 properties ☎ 01263 837672

Loddon

3 cottages at Hardley near
Loddon ☎ 01371 850853

Caravan and Camping Sites

Great Yarmouth

Caravan Club Site (no tents)
☎ 01493 855223

Norwich

**Norfolk Showground
Caravan Club Site**
☎ 01603 742708

Swans Harbour Caravan Park
Marlingford
☎ 01603 759658

Acle

Bureside Holiday Park
☎ 01493 369233

Eating Out

Norwich

Cathedral Restaurant
(closed Sundays)
☎ 01603 471066

Mancroft Octagon, adjacent
to St Peter Mancroft church in
the city centre (closed
Sundays) 01603 610443

Pizza One, Pancakes Too, in
Tombland, an historic part of
Norwich, budget prices
☎ 01603 621583

Adriano's Italian Restaurant
London Street
☎ 01603 622967

Jarrolds Department Store in
the centre has a choice of
three restaurants.

Wroxham

The Old Barn Tearooms at
Wroxham Barns Craft Centre
☎ 01603 784571

Ludham

**Alfresco Restaurant
and Tearoom**
☎ 01692 678384

Events: Norwich & the Norfolk Broads

Great Yarmouth Races
Several meetings each month
throughout the summer.

Caister Carnival
Late June.

Royal Norfolk Show
Early July.

Martham Carnival
Early July.

Bungay Festival
Mid-July.

Beccles Carnival
July/beginning of August.

Stalham Carnival
Early August.

**Great Yarmouth
Carnival Week**
With procession,
mid-August.

Filby Fun Weekend
Late August.

**Norfolk and
Norwich Festival**
Mid-October.

5 BRECKLAND & SOUTH NORFOLK

'The Breckland' is probably less well known to visitors as a distinct part of East Anglia than almost anywhere else in this book. Geographically it occupies the south-western part of Norfolk and a little of north Suffolk. 'The Breckland' is a mixture of grassy heath, pine shelter belts and arable land. Although the underlay is chalk, Breckland is largely covered by windblown sand, with some areas of gravel and boulder clay.

This chapter also includes a part of Norfolk to the south and south-west of Norwich, with pleasant small towns dotted throughout a generally agricultural countryside

A 'breck' was an area of land temporarily cultivated but allowed to revert to heath when its fertility was exhausted.

Thetford to Oxburgh

The most important town of the area and a good place to start is **Thetford**, at the southern end of

Above: Oxburgh Hall

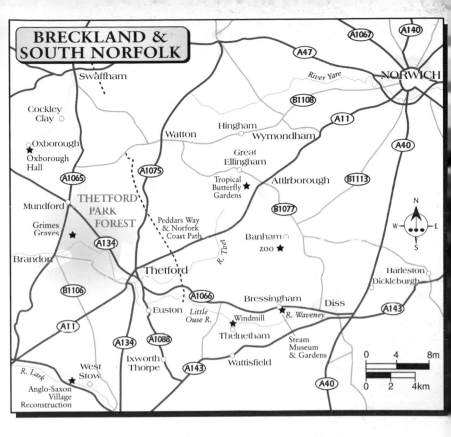

Swaffham

Cockley Clay ○

○ Oxborough
★ Oxborough Hall

A1065

A1075

THETFORD PARK FOREST

Mundford

Grimes Graves ★

A134

Brandon

B1106

Thetford

Peddars Way & Norfork Coast Path

R. Thet

Watton

Hingham ○
Wymondham ○

Great Ellingham

Tropical Butterfly ★ Gardens

Attlrborough

A47

B1108

A11

A40

B1113

B1077

Banham ○
ZOO ★

A1067

A140

NORWICH

River Yare

N
W — E
S

Harleston ○
Dickleburgh ○

A1066

○ Euston

Little Ouse R.

Bressingham

Windmill

Thelnetham

Wattisfield

A134

A1088

Ixworth ○
Thorpe

A143

R. Waveney

Steam Museum & Gardens

Diss

A143

A40

R. Lark

West Stow ○

Anglo-Saxon Village Reconstruction

0   4   8m
0   2   4km

Breckland, by the confluence of the Rivers Thet and Little Ouse, once one of the largest towns in the country. As long ago as the 9th century it was created the capital of a large area invaded by the Danes and was the See of the Bishops of East Anglia until 1091. Although those great days are long past, Thetford is still a busy market town.

Evidence of former greatness is provided by the remains of a 12th century Cluniac Priory, which is only one of a number of religious ruins, and **Castle Hill**, where Iron Age earthworks had a Norman motte and bailey castle superimposed. Castle Hill stands as the largest mound of its kind in East Anglia and in the whole of England only Silbury Hill in Wiltshire is higher. Nearly every street in Thetford has its quota of medieval and Georgian buildings; notable is the 15th century Ancient House in White Hart Street, now in use as a small museum of local history.

The town is the birthplace of Thomas Paine, the great revolutionary and author of 'The Rights of Man'. His gilded bronze statue of 1964 stands outside the Kings House. The **Charles Burrell Museum** is housed in the former painting shop of the famous company which manufactured steam engines and agricultural machinery in the town from 1770 to 1932. The exhibits include recreated workshops and products, working drawings, photographs and much more.

The modern shopping centre is modest but does include a pedestrianised area, linking to a river promenade, with markets on Tuesdays and Saturdays. The railway station has services on the Norwich to Ely and Peterborough line, with connections to

• Thetford Forest •

To the west and north west of the town, Thetford Forest is the overall name given to a large area of woodland, most of it owned and managed by Forest Enterprises. Tree planting started in 1922, with Scots pine predominant. Corsican pine has since taken over as the favoured species but there are also areas of broad leaved trees and of heathland.

Forest Enterprises is noted for a generally 'visitor friendly' attitude and public use and enjoyment of the forest is encouraged, with many car parking and picnic areas and numerous waymarked trails up to 5km (3 miles) in length. The forest was designated as a 'Forest Park' in May 1990. Wildlife includes four types of deer and a small population of our native and much threatened red squirrel.

High Lodge Forest Centre has comprehensive visitor facilities, including play area, cafe, shop and information. Cycle hire is available nearby. The centre is reached via the Forest Drive, a toll road.

Thetford Warren Lodge is quite close to the B1107 road which runs through the forest. It was built about 1400 by the Prior of Thetford for his warrener, the servant who looked after the commercially important rabbit warrens. Once a group of buildings stood here but there was a great deal of damage caused by fire in 1935, leaving just a stark ruin.

Cambridge, London, the Midlands and the North.

On the far side of the forest from Thetford, **Brandon** is a rather ordinary small town. The Heritage Centre in George Street has displays of local history from the stone age, with emphasis on flint knapping, fur and forest industries. Railway services are similar to Thetford but a smaller number of trains stop at Brandon. **Brandon Country Park** is a small part of a former large estate, bought by the Forestry Commission in 1927 and now managed by Suffolk County Council. There is a visitor centre with displays and a small shop. The grounds, including a mausoleum and a walled garden, are available to the public for strolling and for picnics.

Between Brandon and Mundford, still within the overall forest area, is an open expanse covered with the remains of Neolithic flint mines: **Grimes Graves** were first operational some 4000 years ago but were not discovered and excavated until the 1870s. Although of great historic importance, there is not much for the visitor to see without donning a hard hat and descending into the only pit open to the public, 9m (30ft) deep and with a radiating gallery. The site is operated by English Heritage.

Weeting Castle, near Brandon, is also operated by English Heritage. The ruins of a late 12th century moated manor house are incorporated into an 18th century landscaped park, with a domed brick ice house.

A few miles towards Swaffham along the A1065 a left turn leads to **Cockley Cley**, a small village with an inn and an important visitor centre which incorporates a farm museum and a reconstruction of an Iceni village as it is believed to have been at the time of Boudicca, the great warrior queen. A two-storey gate structure gives access to living huts, corn store, chariot house with contemporary chariots and several other buildings.

The story of Roman occupation, Boudicca's rebellion and her final defeat in AD69 is well set out. Included in the same overall site are also a furnished medieval house and St Mary's Chapel, with 7th century origins, incredibly used as a primitive dwelling until 1952. Below the present ground level are the remains of a Roman temple.

Oxburgh Hall is a close neighbour to the west of Cockley Cley. Owned by the National Trust, this lovely moated house of 1482 is set in extensive grounds which include a wilderness garden and woodland walks. Inside the house are atmospheric Victorian interiors, needlework by Mary, Queen of Scots, the armoury, and a 16th century priest's hole. The views from the roof are recommended.

• History of the Breckland •

Human occupation came early to the area because of the easily cultivated light soils; permanent settlement goes back at least 6000 years. As the soils are thin, productivity during medieval times was poor and some of the settlements which were situated furthest from vital water supplies then become deserted. However, large numbers of sheep ensured that the overall economy remained healthy.

The large area of heathland led to the establishment of shooting estates in the 18th and 19th centuries. As these estates declined, much of the land was bought by the then Forestry Commission in the 1920s, the result being the large coniferous forests so evident today.

From prehistoric times there has been a tradition of grazing sheep in large numbers on the open heaths which once covered most of Breckland. Rabbits were introduced by the Normans for their meat and fur, in large warrens surrounded by earthen boundary banks; many banks are still visible in the pine forest.

The soil erosion caused by this intensive grazing resulted in periodic sand blows, contributing to a generally bleak, dry, countryside. The extraction of flint from the chalk for tools and weapons has been carried out for thousands of years. More recently it has been a prime building material in East Anglia generally, often best seen in the numerous fine churches.

This unique combination of geology, previous land use and a drier, more continental, type of climate than is usual in Britain, has resulted in an unusual and surprisingly rich range of plants and animals.

Thetford Priory

English Heritage. Open at any reasonable time.
☎ 01604 730320.

Ancient House Museum

Thetford. Open Jan to May, Monday to Saturday, 10.00 to 12.30, 13.00 to 17.00. June to August, Monday to Saturday, 10.00 to 12.30, 13.00 to 17.00, Sunday, 14.00 to 17.00. Oct to Dec, Monday to Saturday, 10.00 to 12.30, 13.00 to 17.00. Closed at Christmas. ☎ 01842 752599.

Charles Burrell Museum

Thetford. Open from early April to the end of October, Saturday to Monday, 10.00 to 17.00. ☎ 01842 751166.

High Lodge Forest Centre

Thetford Forest Park. Information, cafe and gift shop. Children's play area. Open from Easter to the end of October, 10.00 to 17.00. Winter weekends, 11.00 to 16.00. ☎ 01842 815434.

Brandon Forest Park and Visitor Centre

Gift shop.

Brandon Heritage Centre

Open April to end of May, Saturdays and Bank Holiday Mondays, 10.30 to 17.00, Sundays 14.00 to 17.00. June to August, Thursdays and Saturdays, 10.30 to 17.00, Sundays 14.00 to 17.00. Sept and Oct, Saturday, 10.30 to 17.00, Sunday, 14.00 to 17.00.
☎ 01842 813707.

Grimes Graves

English Heritage. Open from Jan to late March, Wednesday to Sunday, 10.00 to 13.00 and 14.00 to 16.00. Late March to the end of Oct, daily, 10.00 to 13.00 and 14.00 to 18.00 (or dusk in October. November and December, Wednesday to Sunday, 10.00 to 13.00 and 14.00 to 16.00. Closed at Christmas. ☎ 01842 810656.

Weeting Castle

Near Brandon. English Heritage. ☎ 01604 730320.

Cockley Cley Iceni Village and Museums

Disabled access. Gift shop, tearoom and toilets. Open daily from April to end of Oct, 11.00 to 17.30. (Opens at 10.00 during July and Aug). ☎ 01760 721339.

Oxburgh Hall

National Trust. House, gardens, shop and restaurant. Open from late March to the beginning of Nov, daily except Thursday and Friday, 13.00 to 17.00. Bank Holiday Mondays, 11.00 to 17.00. Gardens are also open in March, Saturdays and Sundays, 11.00 to 16.00. Garden, shop and restaurant are open daily in August.

From Watton back to Norwich

Watton sprawls along the B1108, hardly a visitor town but with a Wednesday market and an unusual clock tower dated 1679. The Wartime Museum, with very limited opening hours, tells the story of RAF Watton and the town, 1937-45. Still further to the east, **Hingham** is a pretty market town with greens flanked by narrow streets and Georgian houses.

Continuing to the east, **Wymondham** is a more substantial market town with the magnificent twin-towered abbey church as the principal feature. Also rather special is the timber framed octagonal **market cross**, housing the **Tourist Information Centre**. The oldest inn is the Green Dragon, late 15th century and well placed as a hostelry to serve **Abbey** visitors.

For many centuries the abbey church operated in two parts; the resident monks had the nave, the north aisle and the north-west tower, whilst the townspeople had the remainder. This curious arrangement was, inevitably, caused by a long standing feud. The monastic east end of the great church has gone, but the remainder still offers a great deal to the visitor. Inside, the 15th century nave roof, the 20th century gold altar screen and the triptych

Kett's Rebellion

The brothers who initiated Kett's Rebellion against the enclosure of common land in 1549 were both local men. Having rallied great numbers of peasants against the enclosure of previously common pasture land, they attacked and took the city of Norwich, holding it for some weeks until defeated by superior Government forces.

Robert was hanged at Norwich from the castle walls, William at Wymondham. The oak tree beside which they rallied a large gathering of supporters still lives, with support, by the Wymondham to Hethersett road, B1172.

behind the altar in the north aisle are all particularly good.

The **Bridewell** has a local heritage museum, with exhibits of prison life. Following condemnation of the previous Elizabethan prison, this building housed an early 'model' prison from 1785.

The shopping area includes a fair number of both antique and general shops, with a street market on Fridays.

The **railway station** has been beautifully renovated and now serves two purposes. Its prosaic, everyday, use is to give access to trains for passengers on the Norwich, Ely and Peterborough line. Its other use is to house a railway museum, model railway collection, gift shop and the unusual 'Brief Encounter' themed restaurant.

The Wymondham to East Dereham railway line was finally closed in 1989. It has since been restored by a volunteer organisation and now operates trains as a visitor attraction, with trains running along 18km (11 miles) of line. There are ambitious plans to extend to North Elmham and, eventually, to Fakenham.

The famous **Lotus racing car** organisation has premises close to Wymondham, with limited opening to the public.

Approached through the hamlet of Caister St Edmund on the south side of the A47, Norwich southern ring road, **Venta Icenorum** is 'Norfolk's forgotten town', a comprehensive former Roman town and capital. Almost square, surrounded by large earth banks which are all that remains above ground, the site was opened to the public as recently as 1993. There is plenty of information on site and a car park adjacent.

At **Poringland** the children's attraction 'Play Barn' has farm tours, pony rides and duck pond in addition to the more usual facilities.

To the south-west, on the far side of the A140 at Forncett St Mary, **Forncett Steam Museum** has a collection of large stationary steam engines dating from the early days of steam and now brought back to working order.

Attleborough is a small market (Thursday) town with an interesting church, St Mary's, which was formerly cruciform but has lost its chancel and its apse. The central tower remains and there is some Norman work. The late 15th century rood screen, with painted decoration and a loft, fortunately survived the Reformation. The town has railway services on the Norwich to Ely and Peterborough line.

Three kilometres (2 miles) to the north-west, at **Great Ellingham**, is the **Tropical Butterfly Garden and Bird Park. The tropical gardens** have hundreds of free flying butterflies, falconry displays, conservation area and waterside walk, garden centre, gift shop and coffee shop.

South of Attleborough, **Banham Zoo,** has a collection of big cats (all but lions) shire horses, birds of prey, monkey islands, farmyard corner and fun for children and a choice of restaurants. In total, there are more than 1000 animals and birds on more than 12 hectares (30 acres) of landscaped parkland.

Wymondham Heritage Museum

The Bridewell. Gift shop and tearoom. Open from the beginning of March to the end of November, Monday to Saturday, 10.00 to 16.00. Sunday, 14.00 to 16.00.
☎ 01953 600205.

Wymondham Station

Gift shop and refreshment room (The Brief Encounter). Open daily, 10.00 to 17.00. Sunday, 11.30 to 17.30.
☎ 01953 606433. Note also the restored **Mid-Norfolk Railway** line to East Dereham.
☎ 01362 690633.

Team Lotus

Philip Ford Way, Wymonham. Memorabilia of the famous racing cars. Shop. Open every Wednesday from 09.00 to 17.00.
☎ 01953 603355.

Venta Icenorum

Caister St Edmund on the south side of the A47, Norwich southern ring road. Former Roman town. Open at all reasonable times.
☎ Tourist Information Centre 01953 604721.

Play Barn

Poringland. Open from Easter to October, Monday to Friday, 09.30 to 15.30. Sunday, 10.00 to 17.00.
☎ 01508 495526.

Forncett Steam Museum

Open on the first Sunday each month from May to December, 10.00 to 17.30.
☎ 01508 488277.

Tropical Butterfly Garden and Bird Park

Great Ellingham. Gift shop and coffee shop. Open daily from March to November, 09.00 to 17.30, Sundays 10.00 to 17.30.
☎ 01953 453175.

Banham Zoo

Children's play area. Crafts and shops complex with a pub and other refreshments. Open daily from 10.00 to 15.00 (low season), 16.00 (mid-season), 16.30 (high season).
☎ 01953 887771.

Harleston to Mildenhall

Harleston is a busy commercial centre and market town (Wednesday) with a mellow old market place and a few Georgian houses. King George's Hall in Broad Street houses a local museum.

In the Waveney Valley, right on the boundary between Norfolk and Suffolk, the 110th Bomb Group Memorial Museum at **Dickleborough**, just north of Diss, occupies the control tower of the World War II base from which the group flew B17s. Exhibits comprise photographs, personal stories and memorabilia.

Diss is the most important market town of the area, with an attractive situation on the edge of a 2.5hec (6acre) mere or lake. The church dominates one end of the sloping Market Place, with a pedestrianised shopping street, Mere Street, leading from the top end to the mere. Tudor, Georgian and Victorian buildings, some of them, such as Dolphin House at the top of the Market Place, timber framed, jostle together in the town centre.

Specialist shops can be found in 'yards' off St Nicholas Street, close to the church. As is usual in an old market town, the best features of the buildings can be seen only by looking above the present

Bressingham Gardens – for the gardens, plants and the steam engine centre

day ground floor facades. A small museum in the Market Place has changing displays of the history and pre-history of Diss and its area.

A little way along the Thetford road, Alan Bloom has created one of Norfolk's showpieces at **Bressingham**, a unique mixture of gardens and steam railway museum, now enhanced by fire engines, Victorian roundabout and other attractions. No less than three operational narrow-gauge steam railways compete for custom with the static display of main line standard gauge locomotives from several countries, including a huge 2-10-0 from Norway. Some of the narrow gauge locomotives have their ancestry firmly based in the great quarries of North Wales.

Alan Bloom's Dell Garden is quite beautiful and is bordered by Adrian Bloom's Foggy Bottom Garden. On the far side of the main complex is a two acre plant centre.

Continuing towards Thetford, between the small villages of Blo Norton and **Thelnetham**, Thelnetham Windmill is an early 19th century four floor tower mill driving two pairs of French millstones. Visitors may purchase stone ground floor and other grain products.

Knettishall Heath Country Park is a fine example of Breckland heath and woodland, by the Little Ouse River, with waymarked trails, car park, picnic area, information centre and toilets. The Peddars Way and the Angles Way meet here.

Almost back in Thetford, **Euston Hall** has been the home of the Dukes of Grafton for more than 300 years. Built in the 1660s by Lord Arlington, it was remodelled in the 1750s. Among the contents are portraits by Van Dyck, Lely and Stubbs, the court of King Charles II being particularly featured. The pleasure grounds are by John Evelyn and the park and temple are by William Kent. The 17th century church in the grounds is in the style of Sir Christopher Wren.

To the south-west, near **Lackford** in the valley of the River Lark, **West Stow Country Park and Nature Reserve** is an important centre set in an area of special landscape. Pride of place goes to the reconstruction of an Anglo-Saxon village on its original site, using tools and techniques available to the Anglo-Saxons.

The original village, of about 30 wooden buildings, was partly buried by a 14th century sand-storm. The site is entered via a modern visitor centre. In addition to displays and audio visual programme, there is a museum with objects found during excavations, carried out largely during 1965-72. The complex also has a farm project with animals and crops and a children's play area.

Mildenhall is probably best known as the site where a famous collection of 4th century Roman silverware was found in the early 1940s and, with Lakenheath, as an important World War II centre for the allied bomber squadrons. **Mildenhall and District Museum** is housed in early 19th century cottages in King Street, with modern extensions. Exhibits cover The Royal Air Force presence in the area and the local archaeology and history of Fenland and Breckland. The Church of St Mary and St Andrew has the largest Norman porch in Suffolk.

Places to Visit
From Harleston to Mildenhall

Harleston Museum

Open from early May to late October, Wednesdays 10.00 to 12.00 and 14.00 to 16.00. Saturdays, 10.00 to 12.00.

Diss Museum

Open all year, Wednesday and Thursday, 14.00 to 16.00, Friday and Saturday, 10.30 to 16.30. Closed during Christmas and New Year. ☎ 01379 650618.

100th Bomb Group Memorial Museum

Dickleburgh. Open Saturdays Sundays and Bank Holidays throughout the year, 10.00 to 17.00 (October to April closes at 16.30). ☎ 01553 766089.

Bressingham Steam Museum Trust and Gardens

Shop, garden shop and cafe. Open from April to Septem-

ber, 10.30 to 17.30. October, 10.30 to 16.30. ☎ 01379 687382.

Theltenham Windmill

Sale of flour and other grain products. Open on Bank Holidays and on Sundays from early July to late September, 11.00 to 19.00. ☎ 01359 250622.

Euston Hall

Old Kitchen tea shop, picnic area and craft shop. Wheelchair access to tearoom, craft shop and grounds only. Open on Thursdays from early June to late September and on occasional Sundays, 14.30 to 17.00. ☎ 01842 766366.

Continued on page 126...

Mildenhall and District Museum

King Street. Open from the beginning of March to late December, Wednesdays, Thursdays, Saturdays and Sundays, 14.30 to 16.30. ☎ 01638 716970.

West Stow Country Park and Nature Reserve

Icklingham Road, West Stow. Cafe. Open all year, daily, 10.00 to 17.00 (closed 24th to 26th December). ☎ 01284 728718.

Cycle Rides: Breckland & South Norfolk

The Thetford Forest area is very appealing, using the lesser public roads, preferably in conjunction with waymarked cycle routes within the forest, where the surfaced tracks are also available to cyclists. Cycle Hire is available at the High Lodge Forest Centre.

From the *Norfolk Cycling Map* (produced by Goldeneye Map Guides ☎ 01242 244889), a 55km (35 mile) circuit based on the Upper Waveney Valley links Diss, Redgrave, Thelnetham, East Harling, New Buckenham, Gissing and Diss.

Car Tours: Breckland & South Norfolk

From a Breckland base, anywhere in East Anglia is reachable as a day excursion – just scan the chapters in this book and make your choice. In particular, Cambridge with its manifest attractions is within easy reach.

The Angles Way connects Breckland with Broadland, running for a total of 124km (77 miles), largely along the valley of the River Waveney, visiting Diss, Harleston, Bungay and Beccles. For the Peddars Way, which heads north from the junction with the Angles Way at Knettishall Heath, see Chapter 2.

The **Norfolk Walks** (see Chapter 2) package of leaflets, already mentioned, has village-based walks at Watton, Old Buckenham and Wymondham.

Thetford Forest has no less than 24 generally easy waymarked walks up to a maximum length of 5km (3 miles), all related to car parking areas. At Lynford Arboretum there is an 'easy access trail' accessible to the disabled.

Sculpture in Thetford Forest

Hotels

Wymondham

Wymondham Consort Hotel
☎ 01953 606721

The Abbey Hotel
☎ 01953 602148 Fax 606247

Thetford

The Historic Thomas
Paine Hotel
☎ 01842 755631 Fax 766505

Broom Hall Hotel
Saham Toney
☎ 01953 882125

Diss

Salisbury House
Country Hotel
☎ 01379 740793

The Half-Moon Inn
Rushall
☎ 01379 740793

Inglenook Lodge
Garboldisham
☎ 01953 681541

Mildenhall

Riverside Hotel
☎ 01638 717274 Fax 715997

Guest Houses and B&B

Wymondham

Cobweb Cottage
Queen Street
☎ 01953 604070

Nr Thetford

Colveston Manor
Mundford
☎ 01842 878218 Fax 879218

East Farm, a working arable
farm ☎ 01842 890231
Fax 890457

Rose Cottage
Thompson ☎ 01953 488104

Self-catering

Nr Thetford

Country Cottages
at Roundham Farm
East Harling
☎ 01953 717126 Fax 718593

Diss

Coach and Pump Cottage
and The Olde Laundry
☎ 01379 668146

Caravan and Camping Sites

Nr Thetford

Puddledock Farm
Great Hockham
☎ 01953 498455

The Covert Caravan
Club Site, between Thetford
and Swaffham, no toilet
facilities
☎ 01842 878356

Lowe Caravan Park
Saham Hills, Watton
☎ 01953 881051

Nr Swaffam

Pentney Park Caravan Site
large site 10km (6m) from
Swaffham ☎ 01953 881051

Eating Out

Diss

Salisbury House Restaurant
☎ 01379 644738

Bressingham

**The restaurant at
Bressingham Gardens.**

Wymondham

Brief Encounter at the
station. A working station
but with some buildings
converted into museum and
an intriguing restaurant; well
worth a visit for something
out of the ordinary.

Thetford

The tearoom at Thetford
Forest Visitor Centre.

Public Transport

The Norwich to Peterborough railway line, with connections at
Ely and Peterborough to Cambridge, London, the Midlands,
Scotland and the north-east, passes through Breckland. There
are stations at Wymondham, Attleborough, Harling Road,
Thetford, Brandon and Mildenhall.

The Norwich to Ipswich and London railway line passes
through Diss.

'Sunday Rover' tickets (*see* Chapter 2) are available on many
of the bus routes throughout Breckland and South Norfolk,
involving towns and villages such as Thetford, Bressingham,
Diss, Harleston, Poringland, Attleborough and Wymondham.
☎ Stagecoach United Counties, 01604 620 077.

Events: Fenland

Thetford Forest Park
Activity days throughout the
season. Plays and musical
events in summer.
☎ 01842 815434.

Wymondham Music Week
June, ☎ 01508 533681.

Mildenhall Air Fete
Late May.

Weeting Steam Rally
Mid-July.

6 IPSWICH & THE SUFFOLK COAST

This chapter could well have had the alternative title of 'Suffolk Coasts and Heaths', as most of the area covered lies within the Area of Outstanding Natural Beauty of that name. Much of the AONB is a quite stunning but fragile landscape of 403 square kilometres (156 square miles), stretching roughly from Kessingland to the Stour Estuary, an area treasured for its countryside, wildlife, small villages and towns, with many important habitats. Despite the obvious attraction to visitors, the area remains comparatively uncrowded and relaxed.

Over the centuries of recorded history, the coast has taken a tremendous battering from the elemental power of the North Sea and, despite elaborate coastal defences in modern times, the erosion in areas such as Dunwich has been great. The progressive downward tilting of the southern part of the British Isles is

Above: Waiting for the tide, Walberswick

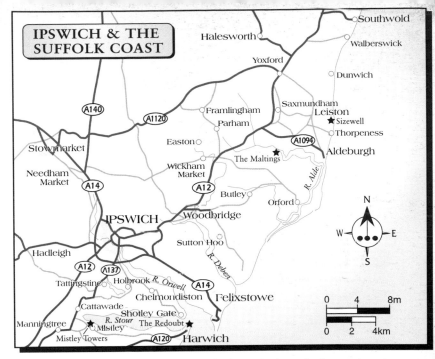

IPSWICH & THE SUFFOLK COAST

predicted to produce a 50cm (1.69ft) relative rise in the sea level by the year 2050 and there is also a possibility of global warming adding to this. It doesn't sound much...but perhaps it would be as well to enjoy the coast and its low lying hinterland whilst we can!

One landscape element which is highly characteristic is the heathland – the Suffolk Sandlings, over 80% of which has been destroyed since the turn of the century. Great efforts are being made to preserve what is left.

This itinerary, starting at Lowestoft and finishing at Ipswich, is very much a coastal route, with occasional inland diversions. It is richly historic, from the early days of tribes such as the Iceni and the Roman conquest, offering the visitor a balance between the attractions of the large towns of Lowestoft and Ipswich, the charms of the smaller towns and villages and the splendour of nature in many forms.

Lowestoft

Britain's most easterly town was, until recently, predominantly a major fishing port. The port is still there, a little way upriver, but a modern seaside resort has been superimposed. The wide, sandy, beaches include an area reserved for naturists. Sea front gardens and a good range of the usual visitor attractions add to the appeal

131

as a family holiday destination.

The shopping centre is quite comprehensive, with some pedestrian areas. Worth a visit is the **East Point Pavilion Visitor Centre**, a striking construction of glass, with imaginative indoor play area for children, large cafe and the **Tourist Information Centre**. To the north of the town centre, **Pleasurewood Hills** is a 20 hec (50acre) complex of rides and other family attractions. Harbour tours, using traditional wooden fishing craft, are yet another attractive proposition.

The **Lowestoft and East Suffolk Maritime Heritage Museum**, The **Lowestoft War Memorial Museum** and the **Royal Naval Patrol Service Association's Naval Museum** are all comparatively small specialised museums, grouped in Sparrow Nest Gardens, Whapload Road. The Maritime Heritage Museum specialises in the history of the Lowestoft fishing fleets, the War Memorial Museum depicts the bombing of Lowestoft in World War II and there is also an aviation room. The third museum is devoted to naval memorabilia, primarily related to the smaller ships such as minesweepers and motor torpedo boats.

A little way inland, **Oulton Broad** is a lovely expanse of water, very much a part of the 'Broads' system of connected waterways. It has been developed for recreational use, with a visitor complex – the Nicholas

Everitt Park of 300 acres, the Yacht Station, hire boats, trips on large launches, water sports, children's play area, tennis, bowls and crazy golf. In the park is the **Lowestoft Museum**, with exhibits which include wartime Lowestoft and a large collection of the famous Lowestoft porcelain. There is an adjacent cafe.

The **International Sailing Craft Association Maritime Museum** in Caldecott Road, on the north edge of the Broad, has a large collection of sailing craft from all over the world.

Lowestoft has no less than three railway stations, including one close to Oulton Broad, with train services to Norwich, Great Yarmouth, Ipswich and London.

At Carlton Colville, on the south-western fringe of the town, the **East Anglia Transport Museum** has buses trams, trolleybuses and other vehicles, some giving short rides and others under cover. Book shop and tearoom complement the exhibits and special weekends are held throughout the season.

Lowestoft to Southwold

To the north of Lowestoft, **Gorleston on Sea** is a sizeable outlier of Great Yarmouth, largely residential, but with a fair array of visitor attractions. Colton is a large linear village with holiday parks.

Hopton on Sea is a great complex of holiday village and static caravan parks, with modern facilities such as shops, cafes, amusement arcades and other entertainment.

Kessingland is a substantial village to the south of Lowestoft, straggling along two minor roads, one of which leads past the church to the sea. There are a few shops, inn and cafes. The beach is stony and not at all pretty, but there is a good variety of sea shore plants.

Most visitors to Kessingland probably come for the **Suffolk Wildlife Park** – 'The African Adventure', with its wide ranging collection of animals housed for the most part in generous open paddocks. Various kinds of lemur are particularly well represented. The protection of endangered species is incorporated into the Park's activities and visitor interest is enhanced by keeper feeding talks. A children's play area, crazy golf and cafeteria supplement the animal collection.

Covehithe is a tiny hamlet with striking evidence of coastal erosion – the little road to the sea terminates very abruptly indeed!

Southwold

Southwold is one of the showplaces of the Suffolk coast, a lovely little town standing above surf-pounded sand and shingle beach, on the site of a Saxon fishing port. The later medieval port suffered from silting and boating activity is now restricted to the mouth of the adjacent River Blyth, where there is a foot ferry across to Walberswick.

The much illustrated lighthouse of 1890 is close to the celebrated Adnams Brewery. Spacious greens now cover the sites of many densely packed houses which were consumed by a great fire in 1659, recorded on a plaque at the Town Hall. The buildings cover a wide range of dates and styles, with Georgian prominent, and a definite Dutch influence. The pink and pale blue so characteristic of Suffolk, is notable. The row of cannons pointing out to sea at Gun Hill is a reminder that the Battle of Sole Bay, fought against the Dutch Fleet in 1672, was close to Southwold.

The tiny Market Place has the fine Swan Hotel and the claimed 'Oldest shop in Town – over 300 years and still going strong with prime, home killed, meat'. Southwold **Sailors' Reading Room** of 1864 appropriately faces the open sea.

Southwold Museum is housed in a listed building in Victoria Street, originally a cottage, condemned as unfit in 1931. The museum was opened in 1933 and has subsequently been extended. Other local exhibits include fishing and model boats, fossils and flints and the Battle of Sole Bay.

East Point Pavilion Visitor Centre

Lowestoft. Restaurant.
☎ 01502 523000.

Pleasurewood Hills

Wheelchair and disabled friendly. Open from 10.00, early April, every day, late April to mid-May, weekends only, mid-May to mid-September, every day, mid-September to early October, every day except Mondays and Fridays. Catering.
☎ 01502 508200.

Maritime Heritage Museum

Lowestoft. Open at Easter weekend, then from late April to October, daily, 10.00 to 17.00.
☎ 01502 561963.

Lowestoft War Memorial Museum

Open early in the year until September, Monday to Friday, 10.00 to 12.00 and 14.00 to 16.30, Sundays 13.30 to 16.30.
☎ 01502 517950.

Naval Museum

Lowestoft. Open early in the year until October, Monday to Friday, 10.00 to 12.00 and 14.00 to 16.30, Sundays, 13.30 to 16.30.
☎ 01502 586250.

Lowestoft Museum at Oulton Broad

Wheelchair access to ground floor. Souvenir shop. Cafe adjacent. Open early to mid-April, Monday to Friday, 10.00 to 17.00, Saturday and Sunday, 14.00 to 17.00. Late April to mid-May, Saturday and Sunday, 14.00 to 17.00. Mid-May to early October, Monday to Saturday, 10.00 to 17.00, Sunday, 14.00 to 17.00. Mid-to late October, Saturday and Sunday, 14.00 to 16.00. Late October to early November, Monday to Friday, 10.00 to 16.00, Saturday and Sunday 14.00 to 16.00. ☎ 01502 511457

Lowestoft Harbour Tours

☎ 01502 574902.

ISCA Maritime Museum

Oulton Broad. Open every day, April to October, 10.00 to 18.00, November to March, 10.00 to 16.00. Closed during Christmas and New Year holidays.

East Anglia Transport Museum

Carlton Colville. Tearooms, book and souvenir shop. Open on Sundays from May to September, 11.00 to 17.30, Mondays to Saturdays during school holidays, 14.00 to 17.00.
☎ 01502 518459.

Suffolk Wildlife Park

Kessingland. Accessible to the disabled; free wheelchair loan. Children's play area. Catering. Open every day except Christmas Day and Boxing Day, January to March and October to December, 10.00 to 16.00. April to June, 10.00 to 17.00. July to September, 10.00 to 17.30.
☎ 01502 740291.

Above:
The lighthouse,
Southwold
Left: Suffolk Wildlife
Park, Kessingland

Southwold Museum

Accessible to the disabled. Open daily from Easter to the end of September, 1430 to 1630. In August, also from 11.00 to 12.30.
☎ Tourist Information Centre 01502 724729.

Blythburgh to Framlingham

Turning inland, the first road crossing of the River Blyth is close to **Blythburgh**, a 15th century port steadily reduced by silting. The great glory here is the magnificent Church of the Holy Trinity, the '**Cathedral of the Marshes**' soaring high above the adjacent low lying land. Building began in 1412; the church has a nave of 37m (127ft) and a lovely clerestory enclosing a tie beam roof. In 1577 the tower was struck by lightening, killing a man and a boy. A 17th century Jack o' the clock and carved bench ends are among the internal features.

Walberswick, facing Southwold across the River Blyth, was another flourishing port. There is a sandy beach. The church of St Andrew is enclosed within the ruins of an older, larger, church. There is a foot ferry across the river.

Returning inland, **Halesworth** is a little town with a railway station on the Lowestoft to Beccles and Ipswich line. The **Halesworth Museum** at the Almshouses, Steeple End also occupies the former fire engine shed. Exhibits include local geology, architecture and local history generally. About 3km (2 miles) north-west are **Wissett Vineyards** at Valley Farm, Wissett, 4hec (10acre) in extent and with a shop for wine tasting.

A shingle beach backed by a large car park marks the spot close to the town of **Dunwich** which has disappeared under the waves. Of the town itself, which reached its peak in the 12th century, there is nothing but the remains of the 13th century Franciscan Friary on the edge of the cliff and the Chapel of the Leper Hospital in the church yard; the advance of the sea was unstoppable.

The story is set out, with the aid of a model, in the nearby Dunwich Museum, which also has a natural history section. The present village appears to have been built a safe distance inland but presumably the medieval town builders felt similarly secure! One and a half kilometres (1 mile) to the south of Dunwich the National Trust has a visitor centre at **Dunwich Heath**, an area of remnants of the formerly widespread sandlings heaths, with walk and access to the beach. The visitor centre has an observation room, tearoom and shop.

Continuing to the south, with access at either Westleton or East Bridge, **Minsmere** is a flagship of the Royal Society for the Protection of Birds, a reserve of national, if not international, importance. The large area of heath, woodland, marsh and lagoon, adjacent to the coast, has nature trails, hides and a comprehensive visitor centre with information, shop and tearoom.

Saxmundham is not very far inland, a quiet market town with some interesting buildings. The church of St John the Baptist has a hammerbeam roof and a 13th century piscina. The Main Street and Market Place have a fair selection of shops, inns and cafes. There is a railway station with services to Lowestoft, Ipswich and beyond.

Further inland, Yoxford and Peasenhall are villages with one long street each and many pretty houses and antique shops. Milestone House in Yoxford has an old milestone as an unusual feature of its front elevation.

Bruisyard is reached by turning right at Rendham. Here, a 4hec (10acre) vineyard is supported by a winery and herb centre, restaurant, gardens and country shop. A tour with audio cassette is offered.

Shawsgate Vineyard is closer to Framlingham, on the B1120. The 6hec (15acre) vineyard has a modern winery, children's play area and light refreshments.

Laxfield lies a few kilometres to the north. The museum is housed in the early 16th century guildhall in the village centre. Featured is the domestic and working life of the village, with displays of archaeology, costume and natural history.

Tannington Hall offers horse and carriage rides along the lanes surrounding the hall, with optional refreshment stops at a local hostelry.

Saxtead Green Postmill is a fine example of a traditional Suffolk postmill, dating from 1776. Production ceased in 1947.

Framlingham is the principal town of this part of rural Suffolk, a market (Saturday) town packed with attractive buildings, crowned by a striking 12th century castle built by Roger Bigod, a member of the powerful East Anglian family. Mary Tudor was proclaimed Queen whilst resident in 1553. The castle, in the care of English Heritage, is remarkably intact, with curtain walls, 13 towers and Tudor brick chimneys. The battlement walk gives fine views over town and surrounding countryside. Within the castle, the Lanman Museum occupies a former poorhouse, with displays concerning the lives of the townspeople over the centuries.

The town centre climbs, steeply for Suffolk, towards the castle, with interesting shops, inns and two groups of almshouses

Framlingham to Felixstowe

The road to the south-east from Framlingham, B1116, leads to Parham; Parham Airfield is close by. The former control tower of the World War II base of the 390th bomb group of the US Air Force has been restored as a memorial museum, with engines and other aircraft parts, documents, paintings and memorabilia.

Halesworth and District Museum

Open from early May to the end of September, Wednesdays, 10.30 to 12.30 and 14.00 to 16.30, Saturdays, 10.30 to 12.30, Sundays and Bank Holidays, 14.30 to 16.30. ☎ 01986 873030.

Dunwich Museum

Open in March at weekends, 14.30 to 16.30, April to September, daily, 11.30 to 14.30, October, 12.00 to 16.00. ☎ 01728 648796.

Minsmere Visitor Centre

Access for the disabled. Tearoom. Open daily except Tuesdays, from 09.00 to 21.00 (or dusk if earlier). ☎ 01728 648281.

Bruisyard Vineyard

Restaurant and tea shop, picnic area and country shop. Open daily except for Christmas and early January, 10.30 to 17.00.

Shawsgate Vineyard

Picnic area, teas and coffees and children's play area. Open daily in summer, 10.30 to 17.00. Check winter opening times. ☎ 01728 724060.

Laxfield and District Museum

Open from the end of May to the end of September, Saturdays, Sundays and Bank Holidays, 14.00 to 17.00. ☎ 01986 798460.

Tannington Hall

About 7km north-west of Framlingham, off the A1120 via Dennington or Saxtead Green. Horse and carriage rides. ☎ 01728 628226.

Saxtead Green Postmill

Open from early March to late October, Monday to Saturday, 10.00 to 13.00 and 14.00 to 18.00. ☎ 01728 685789.

Framlingham Castle

English Heritage. Open daily from January to late March, 10.00 to 16.00. Late March to the end of October, daily, 10.00 to 18.00 (or dusk in October). November and December, daily, 10.00 to 16.00. Closed 24th to 26th December. ☎ 01728 724189.

Opposite top: The Moot House, Aldeburgh Opposite bottom: Sizewell Power Station

On the east side of the main A12 road, the small village of **Snape** is famous for the **Maltings** complex. The adjacent mud flats, reed beds and salt marshes are rich in wildlife. One hour river trips exploring the upper reaches of the River Alde are available from the quay.

Leiston is a small town to the north-east of Snape. The town itself is of limited interest to visitors, but the Leiston Film Theatre on the High Street does claim to be Suffolk's oldest cinema. Formerly of great local economic significance, the extensive factory created by Richard Garrett from 1728 built traction engines and a range of agricultural machinery until closure in 1983, pioneering the use of continuous production line techniques. The Long Shop and some other buildings now comprise a fine museum, thoroughly demonstrating the history and the work of the company.

Leiston Abbey is less than 2km (1.5 miles) north of the town. The considerable ruins of this Premonstratensian monastic foundation include a lay brothers' complex renovated in the 1980s to house a music school and concert hall.

Sizewell, just down the road from Leiston comprises two major nuclear power stations, one old and one comparatively new. The great dome is a major landmark. There is a comprehensive visitor centre, with tours of both stations. Adjacent to the power stations is the Sizewell Belts area, with way-marked nature trails. Sizewell beach is only a short walk from the station car park.

Thorpeness is an unusual place. Planned from 1910 by G. S. Ogilvie, it focuses on the Meare, a shallow lake 26hec (64acres) in extent used for various kinds of boating and other activities. Other buildings in various styles and a golf course were added, to create a holiday village with inn, coffee shop and country club.

Bizarre, even by Thorpeness standards, is the **'House in the Clouds'** of 1923. A huge water tower, with accommodation below, its tank was converted into extra accommodation when mains water came to the village in the 1960s. The windmill opposite this strange house was moved from Aldringham to pump water up to the tank, likewise becoming redundant.

Aldeburgh is another of the very special places on the Suffolk coast particularly, but by no means exclusively, for those who love music. Spread along the edge of the sea behind a shingle beach, with a long shopping street in parallel, this small town has many charming buildings and vistas and, above all, that indefinable quality, atmosphere. Small fishing boats are drawn up on the shingle and their catches are sold from nearby huts exactly as they were many years ago. Benjamin Britten lived here for 30 years in a house not far from the celebrated Moot Hall, marked by a plaque.

Another local celebrity, Elizabeth Garrett Anderson is commemorated in the attractive and interesting church. A native of Aldeburgh, she was the first woman physician and surgeon and also the first woman in Britain to hold the office of Mayor. In addition to Britten, his lifelong companion, the tenor Peter Pears, and Imogen Holst, daughter of another major composer, are buried here. Don't miss the commemorative window by John Piper. The poet George Crabbe was born in Aldeburgh and was curate for a short time.

The **Moot Hall**, of Tudor origin, is probably Aldeburgh's best known building, standing alone with the sea creeping closer over the centuries. The building is still used as the town hall and also as a local museum, including objects from the Snape ship burial, which pre-dates the more famous burial at Sutton Hoo.

The lowest road crossing of the River Alde is by Snape Maltings. A turn towards the sea leads to **Orford**, another place with Britten musical associations. A busy port when the castle was built by King Henry II in 1165, but now cut off from the sea by the great expansion of the shingle spit of Orford Ness, Orford is much more of a backwater. Of the castle, only the cylindrical keep remains, standing guard over the brick and timber cottages below. Inside are magnificent rooms.

Market Hill rises through the tiny town, with its inns, restaurants and shops. At the top, the flint church of St Bartholomew was an important part of the early days of the Aldeburgh Festival. Britten's operas such as *Noye's Fludde* and the three church parables were all premiered here. There is an appropriate floor plaque to the composer.

Boat trips operate from the quay, including a circuit of Havergate Island in the estuary,

The Maltings

Snape Maltings was once a busy industrial site with a quay from which malt was sent by barge to London and Norwich; a railway line constructed in 1859 took over much of the trade.

In 1968, the composer Benjamin Brittain took the lead in the conversion of the then redundant maltings to the Jubilee Hall, the principal concert hall for the celebrated Aldeburgh Festival. There is now a year long programme of diverse events in the hall, including an Easter Festival and the Snape Proms, in August.

Recently, other maltings buildings have been refurbished to provide a range of specialist shops, including crafts, house and garden, books and antiques, with inn and tea shop.

managed by the Royal Society for the Protection of Birds and noted for its avocets. Brunch, lunch and dinner cruises are available on the *Lady Florence*, a 50ft, ex-Admiralty motor vessel, equipped with a cosy coal fire in winter.

There is also a ferry across to Orford Ness, where the National Trust has displays of the history and natural history of the Ness, the largest vegetated shingle spit in Europe. The great variety of habitats support a significant number of rare species and rare plant communities. Guided walks and self-guided trails, with booklets, are available. Access is by ferry from Orford Quay. **Orford Museum**, tucked away behind the Crown and Castle Hotel, has a small local collection.

Wickham Market is a small, quiet, unpretentious town, with a railway station nearby. **Valley Farm Carmargue Horses** claims to have Britain's only herd of breeding Carmargue horses. **Easton Farm Park**, about 3km (2 miles) to the north-west, is a Victorian model farm with dairy centre, Suffolk horses, pets paddock, green trail beside the River Deben and other attractions.

Heading south, **Woodbridge**, 15km (9 miles) from the sea, on the estuary of the River Deben, has much to offer the visitor. The waterfront, backed by the railway line, is fascinating: boatyards, boat builders, chandlery stores and sailmakers have jostled for space for six centuries, resulting in a pleasing hotch-potch which includes some really old buildings. Pride of place goes to the weatherboarded tide mill of 1793. After closure in 1957, the mill was restored and reopened 1973. Operation of the machinery is dependant on tide levels.

• Benjamin Britten •

Born at Lowestoft in 1913, Benjamin Britten soon became one of the bright stars in the British musical firmament of his time. By the age of 12 years he was sponsored by noted musicians, first Frank Bridge and later by John Ireland. By 1930 he had entered the Royal College of Music and by 1933 his *opus 1* was published.

Through the 1930s he composed a good deal of incidental music, moving to the United States of America in 1939 and then to Aldeburgh in 1942. This small coastal town became his actual and spiritual home for the rest of his life.

The rise to fame after World War II was rapid, with the production of modern music accessible to the average listener. In 1945 the opera *Peter Grimes* sealed that fame; a totally new voice in music of international stature; dark and beautiful music, evoking the wind keening over the restless sea of the Suffolk coast as no composer has done before or since. Britten's empathy with his Aldeburgh environment and with the words of George Crabbe's poem *The Borough* came together to inspire him and to raise his work to a lofty pinnacle.

At the same time, Britten was active in helping to found the English Opera Group, which premiered many of his works and, with his life partner Peter Pears, in founding the Aldeburgh Festival, an annual musical event of international importance. The festival has always been diffused among Suffolk venues: Orford Church, Blythburgh Church and, in the early days, the Jubilee Hall in Aldeburgh have all been heavily involved. The renovation and conversion of an old maltings building at Snape gave the festival a more substantial and permanent concert hall.

Compositions of this era include the cheerful *Spring Symphony* of 1949, the operas largely for children – *The Little Sweep* and *Noye's Floode*; the three church parables stylistically much influenced by Japanese Noh plays; the 1953 opera *Gloriana* on the life of Queen Elizabeth I and the grim *War Requiem* written for the reopening of Coventry Cathedral in 1962.

Since his death in 1976 his popularity has waned a little, but there is no doubt that his profundity, allied to brilliant technique, will maintain his eminent position in 20th century British music. Certainly no one has written more expertly and joyously for boys' voices.

Red House, his home in Aldeburgh for two decades, carries a plaque; both Orford and Aldeburgh Churches also have memorials to the musical composer who contributed so much towards the enduring popularity of this previously little known area, but his best memorial is the continuing success of the Aldeburgh Festival.

The plaque to Benjamin Britten, Aldeburgh

BENJAMIN BRITTEN
O.M.,C.H.
1913-1976
Composer
Freeman of Aldeburgh
Lived and worked here
1947-1957

The main street rises to **Market Hill**, a small square, where Shire Hall, with its curly Dutch gables, is dominant. Inside is the **Suffolk Horse Museum**. The adjacent ornate pump and drinking trough is dated 1876.

Close by is the parish church of St Mary the Virgin, reached by cobbled pathways. The porch and the decorations of square dressed flint are particularly good. **Woodbridge Museum** is in Market Hill. Local history and the Anglo-Saxon site at **Sutton Hoo** are featured. Although the treasure is in the British Museum, the site of the famous ship burial can

Sutton Hoo Ship Burial

In 1939 excavations at a group of grassy burial mounds overlooking Woodbridge and the River Deben revealed evidence of an Anglo-Saxon longship containing the treasure believed to have belonged to an early English king, Raedwald of East Anglia, who died around AD625.

The ship's timbers were completely rotted away, but the position of the nails revealed it to have been 24-27m (80-90ft) in length and over 4m (14ft) wide. No bones have been found but the treasure is the richest ever found in this country.

As war was imminent, the relics were carefully stored until 1945 when they were cleaned and restored for display in the British Museum in London. The treasure includes an iron helmet, gilded shield, bowls and spoons, purse with coins, clasps, buckles and a musical instrument.

be visited. It is signposted off the B1083 road towards Bawdsey, opposite the junction to Hollesley. From the road there is a well-signposted walk of about 1.6km (1 mile), 20 minutes, to reach the site.

Buttram's Mill is situated close to the A12 main road as it by passes the town centre. Over 18m (60ft) in height, its six floors are packed with milling machinery and the sails turn on suitable days. The mill is privately owned but is maintained and opened to the public by Suffolk County Council.

Between Woodbridge and the sea, **Rendlesham Forest** is a large and important woodland area, with cycle trails and forest walks.

Felixstowe is a sizeable town along the sea coast between the estuaries of the Rivers Deben and Orwell. It has developed as a family holiday resort, with sand and shingle beach backed by sloping gardens and some of the usual amusement park attractions, pier and the Spa Pavilion Theatre.

Inland is a shopping centre and a railway station at the end of a branch line which connects to main line services at Ipswich. The port of Felixstowe, now one of the largest modern container ports in Britain, is adjacent. Ferry services ply between Harwich, Felixstowe and Shotley and also across the River Deben between Bawdsey and Felixstowe.

Landguard Point has, at least since Roman times, been regarded as of strategic defensive importance, hence the succession of forts built, rebuilt and superimposed on this site. King Henry VIII contributed to the development of the fort. As seen today, the fort is substantially as built in 1844, although the red brick walls are of 1744. The **Felixstowe Museum** is housed in nine rooms of the Ravelin block of the fort; the exhibits include a Roman collection, local history, naval room and a recreated village store.

Between the Estuaries

To the south of Ipswich is a peninsula between the estuaries of the Orwell and the Stour. At Chelmondiston a left turn leads to **Pin Mill**, where the Waterside Inn, the adjacent boatyard and the various old barges all contribute to an authentic marine environment, beloved of the writer Arthur Ransome. At the tip of the peninsula is Shotley Gate, formerly the home of *HMS Ganges*, the well known Royal Naval Training Establishment. Returning inland, the Royal Hospital School, near Holbrook, has a grandiose tower and at Tattingstone a row of farm cottages has been shaped, including the provision of a tower at one end, in a deliberate attempt to make the whole structure look like a church.

• Arthur Ransome •

Many people are surprised to discover that this much-loved children's writer has strong East Anglian connections. His most famous classic *Swallows and Amazons* is set in the Lake District, at the other end of the country – although water and boats are a constant theme in his books. The Ransomes were an East Anglian family, with roots traced as far back as the 16th century.

Arthur was born in Leeds in 1884; his father was a professor at the Yorkshire College, now the University of Leeds, spending much of his leisure time in the Lake District, not very far away. This was sheer bliss for young Arthur, roaming freely with other children whilst his father fished.

After boarding school and a very short university career, Arthur lived in London as a journalist, soon starting to write books. He returned from a spell as a war correspondent in Russia to settle in a cottage near Windermere with his second wife, Evgenia.

A great deal of sailing, involving the children of his close friends, the Altounyans, provided the inspiration for *Swallows and Amazons*, published in 1930, the turning point of his career. After writing several sequels, the Ransomes decided to move to the east coast in 1935 for health reasons, renting Broke Farm, Levington, across the estuary of the River Orwell from Pin Mill. They bought a boat and became part of the Pin Mill sailing community. Many holidays were spent sailing on the Norfolk Broads.

In 1939 they moved across the river to live at Harkness Hall but the disturbance of the war soon motivated a return to the Lake District. A post war attempt to find a suitable house in Suffolk was unsuccessful and for the remaining years of their lives the Ransomes shuttled between London and Lakeland. Arthur died in 1967, Evgenia seven years later.

The twelve adventure story books for children have become classics, with a large and loyal following of adults. The books are set in both the Lake District and the east coast Norfolk Broads. Whilst those in the former are jumbled and not literal in their settings, those involving such places as Horning Ferry, Potter Heigham, Oulton Broad and Pin Mill are accurately depicted. The books set in East Anglia are: *Racundra's First Cruise; Peter Duck; Coot Club; We Didn't Mean to go to Sea; Secret Water; The Big Six.*

390th Bomb Group Memorial Museum

Parham Airfield. Souvenir shop and refreshments. Open from early March to late October, Sundays, 11.00 to 18.00. Also on Wednesdays during June to August, 11.00 to 16.00.
☎ 01473 711275.

The Visitor Centre, Sizewell B Power Station

Snape Maltings

Catering.
☎ 01728 688930.

Long Shop Museum

Leiston. Open from the beginning of April to the end of October, Mondays to Saturdays, 10.00 to 17.00, Sundays, 11.00 to 17.00.
☎ 01728 832189.

Sizewell Visitor Centre

For details of opening hours and times of tours.
☎ 01728 653890.

Thorpeness Windmill

Open at Easter from 14.00 to 17.00 and on Saturdays, Sundays and Bank Holiday Mondays during May, 11.00 to 13.00 and 14.00 to 1700. July and August, Monday to Friday, 14.00 to 17.00, Saturdays and Sundays, 11.00 to 13.00. September, 11.00 to 13.00 and 14.00 to 17.00.

Moot Hall Museum

Aldeburgh. Open from Easter to November. April and May weekends, 14.30 to 17.00. June to September and October, daily, 14.30 to 17.00, July and August, daily, 10.30 to 12.30 and 14.30 to 17.00. ☎ Tourist Information Centre.

Cruises on Lady Florence

Orford. ☎ 0831 698 298.

Orford Ness

Open from Easter to the end of October, Thursday, Friday and Saturday.
☎ 01394 450057.

Easton Farm Park

Near Wickham Market. Gift shop, adventure playground, licensed tearoom and picnic area. Open from late March to the end of September, 10.30 to 18.00, daily except Mondays. Open on Bank Holiday Mondays and Mondays in July and August.

Woodbridge Museum

Open from Easter to the end of October, Thursday to Saturday and Bank Holidays, 10.00 to 16.00, Sundays, 14.30 to 16.30. School Summer Holidays, open all week except Wednesdays.
☎ 01394 380502.

Suffolk Horse Museum

Woodbridge. Difficult for the disabled. Open from Easter Monday to the end of September, 14.00 to 17.00.
☎ 01394 380643.

Buttram's Mill

Woodbridge. Open from May to September, Saturdays, Sundays and Bank Holidays, 14.00 to 18.00.
☎ 01473 583352.

Woodbridge Tide Mill

Open at Easter and daily from the beginning of May to the end of September, Saturdays and Sundays in October, 11.00 to 17.00.
☎ 01473 626618.

Sutton Hoo

Near Woodbridge. National Trust. Guided tours. Open from Easter to the end of October, Saturday, Sunday and Bank Holiday Monday afternoons. Guided tours commence at 14.00.
☎ 01394 411288.

Felixstowe Museum

Museum shop and light refreshments. Open on Easter Sunday and Monday, each Sunday in April, and every Sunday and Wednesday from May to September, 14.00 to 17.00. ☎ 01394 286403.

Ferries

Felixstowe to Harwich
☎ 0589 371138.

Bawdsey to Felixstowe
☎ 01728 724160.

Ipswich

Ipswich is a large, vibrant, town in the south-east corner of Suffolk, running Norwich close in its appeal to visitors. It is a very old town and port on the River Orwell, established by the Anglo-Saxons, raided by the Vikings and with a charter conferred by King John in AD1200. The great Cardinal Wolsey, Chancellor of England, was the son of an Ipswich butcher.

Twelve medieval churches, including one used by the Tourist Information Centre, stand as testimony to the town's size and historic importance. The present parish church is St Mary le Tower, in Tower Street. **Cornhill**, the ancient market place and focal point of the Anglo-Saxon street layout, is now bounded by the Italianate town hall, Lloyds Bank and the post office.

The shopping centre is comprehensive, much of it pedestrianised and with modern indoor complexes such as the Buttermarket Centre. One of the more notable town centre features to look out for when strolling is **The Old House** which has, arguably, the finest wall pargetting in East Anglia.

The White Horse Hotel in Tavern Street hides an early 16th century structure behind its Georgian facade. In Lady Lane the modern **Wolsey Theatre** provides quality entertainment; other theatres are the Ipswich Regent Theatre in St Helens Street and the Ipswich Film Theatre located inside the Corn Exchange.

Christchurch Park is a spacious area right on the edge of the town centre. At the heart of the park is a splendid Tudor mansion of 1549, on the site of a former priory. The Mansion houses a fine collection of British pottery, porcelain and glassware, whilst the **Suffolk Artists' Gallery** includes the largest collection outside London of paintings by Thomas Gainsborough and John Constable, in addition to many by other fine artists.

Returning towards the town centre, look out for St Mary's Church, part 13th but mainly 15th century, the Packhorse Inn, facing the Mansion and, in Northgate Street, Pykenham's Gatehouse of 1471. Nearby Oak House was formerly the Royal Oak Inn, of the 15th and 16th centuries but much restored.

Ipswich Museum is sited in High Street, featuring local history from Anglo-Saxon times, geology and wildlife including a bird collection. **Ipswich Transport Museum**, situated in Cobham Road, east of the town centre, occupies a depot built in 1937 to house the trolleybus fleet.

Rather unusual is the **Tolly Cobbold Brewery Museum** in Cliff Road. Established in the 18th century and rebuilt in the 1890s this traditional brewery offers guided tours and a brewery shop.

Places to Visit
In & Around Ipswich

Ipswich Museum

Wheelchair access to ground floor; stair lift to first floor. Museum shop. Open daily except 24th to 26th. December, 1st January and Good Friday, Tuesday to Saturday, 10.00 to 17.00.
☎ 01473 213761.

Christchurch Mansion

Ipswich. Access for the disabled to most of the ground floor and the Wolsey Art Gallery. Open from April to October, Tuesday to Saturday, 10.00 to 17.00, Sunday, 14.30 to 16.30. November to March, closes at 16.10. Closed Good Friday, 24th to 26th December and New Year's Day. Open most Bank Holiday Mondays.
☎ 01473 253246.

Ipswich Transport Museum

All areas are wheelchair accessible. Tearoom and gift shop. Open every Sunday and Bank Holiday Monday from mid-April to late October, 11.00 to 16.30. During August also Monday to Friday, 13.00 to 16.00.
☎ 01473 715666.

Tolly Cobbold Brewery Tours

Ipswich. For details, ☎ 01473 231723.

 ## Car Tours: Ipswich & the Suffolk Coast

No particular recommendations as the whole of the southern part of East Anglia is within reach. Construct your own itineraries from the information in this book.

Public Transport

Railways comprise the Norwich to Ipswich and London main line, the Lowestoft to Norwich line and the Ipswich to Bury St Edmonds, Ely, Cambridge and Peterborough lines.

The 'Suffolk Linkline' ticket, issued and used by two railway companies and two bus companies, permits train and bus linked journeys into and out of Ipswich from a number of Suffolk stations on one ticket, at a small discount. Ipswich Buses, ☎ 01473 232600. Eastern Counties Buses, ☎ 01473 253734.

Walks: Ipswich & the Suffolk Coast

The **Suffolk Coastland and Heaths Path** runs for 80km (50 miles) from Lowestoft to Felixstowe, with many possibilities to construct shorter circular walks using parts of this linear trail.

Rendlesham Forest, east of Woodbridge is well provided with waymarked footpaths, car parking and picnic sites, toilets and adventure play area. The **Tangham Phoenix Trail** has a section suitable for disabled and visually impaired visitors.

Butley Corner picnic site on the B1084 has a car park and another waymarked trail.

Suffolk County Council has prepared and issued, via Tourist Information Centres, a good series of low priced leaflets setting out walks in some of the interesting places and areas. Countryside Walks includes two walks based on Snape, whilst Heritage Coast Walks include Dunwich and Southwold. Most of the walks are quite short, typically 2 to 7km (1.5 to 4miles).

Adjacent to **Sizewell Power Station**, four colour coded walks through the Kenton and Goose Hills area are surprisingly attractive.

Orford Ness has a choice of marked trails and a 7km (4 mile) pedestrian access route.

 # Cycle Rides: Ipswich & the Suffolk Coast

The **Suffolk Coastal Cycle Route** is a circuit visiting many places featuring in the southern area of this chapter, including Felixstowe, Woodbridge, Framlingham, Bruisyard, Snape Maltings and Orford. Leaflets available from Tourist Information Centres.

Rendlesham Forest has recommended cycle rides, including the Three Forest Cycle Route of 39km (24 miles), based on the main car parks.

The railways of this part of East Anglia have helpful policies concerning the carriage of cycles.

CYCLE HIRE

Suffolk Cycle Centre
211, London Road South,
Lowestoft.
☎ 01502 585968.

Byways Bicycles
Priory Farm, Darsham,
Saxmundham.
☎ 01728 668764.

Martlesham Pedal Power
The Square, Marsham.
☎ 01473 610500.

Felixstowe Pedal Power
113, High Road, West Felixstowe.
☎ 01394 286900.

Tangham Forest
☎ as Martlesham.

Hotels

Hintlesham

Hintlesham Hall
One of the most luxurious hotels in the country with leisure club and golf course
☎ 01473 652268 Fax 652463

Ipswich

Forte Posthouse
London Road, large modern hotel with 110 rooms
☎ 01473 690313 Fax 680412

The Marlborough Hotel
Henley Road, luxury hotel with 22 rooms
☎ 01473 257677
Fax 226927

Southwold

The Swan, well known hotel right in the centre, 45 rooms
☎ 01502 722186 Fax 724800

The Crown
☎ 01502 722275 Fax 727263

Woodbridge

The Crown
☎ 01394 384242

Orford

The Crown and Castle
☎ 01394 450205 Fax 450176

Lowestoft

Parkhill Hotel
☎ 01502 730322 Fax 731695

Oulton Broad

Ivy House Farm Hotel
☎ 01502 501353 Fax 501539

Aldeburgh

The Wentworth Hotel
☎ 01728 452312 Fax 454343

Guest Houses and B&B

Nr Aldeburgh

Park Farm
Sibton ☎ 01728 668324
Fax 668564

Nr Southwold

Manor Farm
Uggeshall
☎ 01502 578546 Fax 578560

Hintlesham

College Farm
600 acre working farm
☎ and Fax 01473 652253

Nr Woodbridge

Watersmeet
Laxfield
☎ 01986 798880

Nr Framleigh

Colston Hall
Badingham,
Elizabethan farmhouse
☎ 01728 638375

Woodlands Farm
Brundish ☎ 01379 384444

Self-catering

Southwold

Richard and Wendy Pither
☎ 01379 651297

Aldeburgh

Letheringham Lodge
Letheringham
☎ 01728 748133 Fax 668564

Caravan and Camping Sites

Lowestoft

Beach Farm Caravan and Camping
large site 2 miles south of Lowestoft ☎ 01502 572794

Four Acres Caravan Site at Carlton Colville 3 miles south-west of Lowestoft
☎ 01502 572026

Nr Woodbridge

The Moon and Sixpence Caravan Park
Waldringfield
☎ 01473 736650

Leiston

Cake and Ale Caravan Park
☎ 01728 831655

Ipswich

Low House Touring Caravan Park
Foxhall, 3 miles from Ipswich
☎ 01473 659437

Nr Beccles

Beulah Hall Caravan Site
Mutford ☎ 01502 476609

Saxmundham

Carlton Park Caravan and Camping
(Saxmundham Sports Club)
☎ 01728 604413

Eating Out

Hintlesham

Hintlesham Hall
Considered to be one of the best restaurants in the whole of England ☎ 01473 652268 Fax 652463

Orford

The Old Warehouse Cafe
Quay Street ☎ 01394 450210

Woodbridge

Mrs Piper's Tearooms
The Thoroughfare
☎ 01394 385633

Ipswich

Wolsey's Restaurant at the Ipswich County Hotel
☎ 01473 209988

Felixstowe

The Wolsey Restaurant
at The Waverley Hotel
☎ 01394 282811

Dunwich Heath

The Tearoom at the Coastguard Cottages (National Trust)
☎ 01728 648505

Aldeburgh Easter Festival

Late March/early April.

Easter Fair

Seafront, Felixstowe. Late March/early April.

Lowestoft Spring Fair

At North Denes. Late April.

Suffolk Show

Suffolk Showground, Ipswich. Late May.

Felixstowe Drama Festival

Late May.

Trinity Fair

Southwold
Early June.

Lowestoft Maritime Heritage Week

Mid-June.

Aldeburgh Festival

Mid-to late June.

Maritime Ipswich

Mid-June.

Classic Boat and Beer Festival

Ipswich. Late June/early July. Framlingham Horse Show Mid-July.

Lowestoft Seafront Air Festival

Late July.

Aldeburgh Summer Theatre

August.

Snape Proms

August.

Lowestoft Carnival

Early August.

Ipswich Carnival

August.

Felixstowe Carnival

Mid-August.

Aldeburgh Carnival

Mid-August.

Oulton Broad Regatta Week

Late August.

Grand Henham Steam Rally

Henham Park nr. Blythburgh. Mid-September.

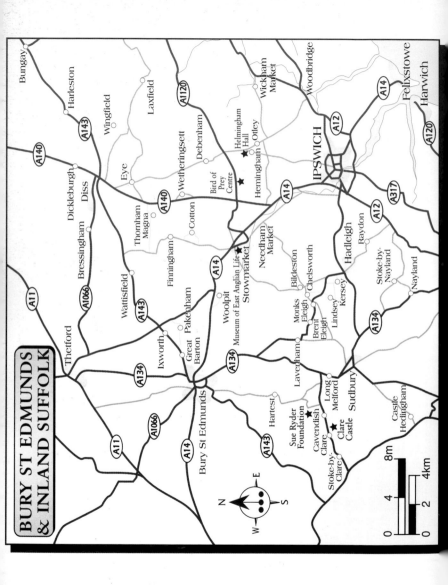

BURY ST EDMUNDS
& INLAND SUFFOLK

Bungay
Harleston
Wingfield
Laxfield
A143
A140
Dickleburgh
Diss
Eye
Wetheringsett
A120
Debenham
Helmingham Hall
Otley
Wickham Market
Woodbridge
IPSWICH
A14
A12
Felixstowe
Harwich
A120
A317
Bird of Prey Centre
Hemingham
A140
Cotton
Thornham Magna
Bressingham
A11
A1066
Wattisfield
A143
Finningham
Needham Market
Stowmarket
Museum of East Anglian Life
Bildeston
Chelsworth
Hadleigh
Raydon
A12
Stoke-by-Nayland
Nayland
Thetford
Ixworth
Woolpit
Great Barton
A14
A134
Monks Eleigh
Brent Eleigh
Lindsey
Kersey
A134
A1066
A134
Lavenham
Long Melford
Sudbury
Castle Hedingham
A11
Bury St Edmunds
A14
Hartest
Sue Ryder Foundation
Cavendish
Clare
Clare Castle
A143
Stoke-by-Clare

N
E
S
W

8m
4
0
4km
2
0

154

7 BURY ST EDMUNDS & INLAND SUFFOLK

Inland Suffolk has a reputation as a quiet and un-eventful part of England, a place where a slower pace of life is the envy of those who live more stressful lives. Less kindly, others might say that it is a rural backwater where peasants with straw behind their ears might still be found.

It is certainly true that outside bustling towns like Bury St Edmunds and Haverhill the pace of life is slow. However, cultivation on the large, highly mechanised farms is hardly the rural idyll depicted by local painter John Constable, and farm workers are outnumbered by tractors and combine harvesters. It could also be argued that the various tourism bodies, in their efforts to bring visitors and money into the county, are themselves in danger of reducing the peace and calm which is such a prime asset.

Having said that, much of rural Suffolk is lovely. Without real hills, but seldom boringly flat, the countryside rolls pleas-antly, with vistas changing as

Above: Cavendish village

155

you travel along the quiet roads. Sometimes nestling in river valleys, sometimes sitting more boldly elevated, the small towns and the villages bear comparison with any in the country.

The medieval wool trade brought great wealth to Suffolk, when Lavenham ranked 14th in the league table of wealthy English towns and the population of the county was relatively high. This prosperity produced a legacy of fine houses and, above all in every sense, lavishly decorated churches of extravagant size for which Suffolk is famous.

Much of the feel of bygone Suffolk has been captured for posterity by East Anglian painters. John Constable and Thomas Gainsborough are the best known but by no means the only great contributors, as a visit to the Castle Museum at Norwich will confirm.

The itinerary suggested here weaves its way seductively through the area, starting and finishing at Bury St Edmunds, visiting virtually every site of visitor interest, be it the quiet contemplation of the hammer beam roof of a wool church, patting the heads of rare farm animals or the excitement of riding behind a hard puffing steam locomotive on a preserved railway line.

Bury St Edmunds

The principal town of inland Suffolk, as it has been since well before records began, Bury St Edmunds was chosen in the 7th century as a suitable place for a monastery. Rather more than 200 years later it became the final resting place for the body of King Edmund

Since dissolution of the monasteries by King Henry VIII, most of the Abbey has disappeared or been incorporated into other buildings. Remaining are two great gateways and much of the west front, including the Norman Samson's Tower, all set in well tended gardens beside the present cathedral. The west front houses a **visitor centre** with displays of the Abbey's history.

Suffolk's only **cathedral** stands close by. Construction of the nave commenced in 1510 on the site of one of the churches which had been part of the Abbey. The cathedral is light and airy inside, with fine roof work and much else of interest, not least the fact that the building is still unfinished. At the top of the treasury stairs the crucifixion statue is by Elizabeth Frink. Another interesting church, St Mary's is immediately to the south of the cathedral.

The compact town centre is busy, with the shopping area centred on the Market Place (markets each Wednesday and Saturday). Dating from 1180, and claimed to be the oldest surviving house in England, **Moyse's Hall**, in the town centre, has been a museum since 1899. The

King Edmund

Edmund, young King of the East Angles, was captured by Danish raiders in 870. They offered to spare his life if he would renounce Christianity. He refused and died a horrible death, being beaten then tied to a tree and shot full of arrows, finally his head was cut off and flung into a wood.

Legend says his followers, searching for the head so it could be buried with the body, heard a voice saying "Here, here" and found the head, guarded by a huge wolf.

Edmund was buried for 33 years at Hoxne where he had died, miracles were soon attributed to him and he was canonised. His body was moved to Beodricksworth Monastery in 903. The Danish King Canute repaid the havoc wrought by his forefathers by founding an abbey in Edmund's name in 1032. The abbey rapidly became a place of pilgrimage and by 1065 Beodricksworth had become St Edmunds Bury.

undercroft has Norman arches. The collection includes archaeology and local history.

Manor House Museum is a restored Georgian mansion, housing paintings, ceramics, clocks and watches from the 17th to the 20th centuries. Robert Adam's only public building in the east of England houses the Bury St Edmunds **Art Gallery**. The magnificent cruciform upper floor is used for a programme of changing exhibitions. At the far end of Crown Street, the **Theatre Royal** of 1819 is a little gem, the third oldest surviving theatre in Britain, with a Regency interior. It is owned by the National Trust and open to the public as a low key visitor attraction.

On the northern edge of town, close to the railway station and beside Tesco, the **Hospital of St Saviour** was a 12th century foundation built by the Abbey to house elderly monks. It was largely demolished in 1539, leaving only traces of the former structures. The site was recently excavated, yielding much of interest.

There is a railway station on the line connecting Ipswich and Ely, where there are connections to Cambridge and London and to Peterborough, the Midlands and the North.

Pakenham to Wingfield College

Leave Bury St Edmunds and head north-east, towards Ixworth. A

Abbey Visitor Centre

Access for wheelchairs. Open April and October, daily, 10.00 to 17.00. May and September, daily, 10.00 to 18.00. June to August, daily, 10.00 to 20.00. November to March, Wednesday and Saturday, 10.00 to 16.00, Sunday, 12.00 to 16.00.
☎ 01284 763110.

Moyse's Hall Museum

Access for wheelchairs to ground floor only. Open all year, Monday to Saturday, 10.00 to 17.00, Sunday, 14.00 to 17.00.
☎ 01284 757488.

Manor House Museum

Access for wheelchairs. Shop and tearoom. Open from Tuesday to Saturday, 10.00 to 17.00, Sunday, 14.00 to 17.00. Open on Bank Holiday Mondays.

Theatre Royal

Westgate Street. National Trust, working theatre. Open daily from 10.00 to 20.00, except Sundays. Closed every Bank Holiday except for performances. Check in advance for theatre opening.
☎ 01284 755469.

Frink's statue of Edmund at Bury St Edmund

diversion to the right at Great Barton leads to **Pakenham**, where a restored watermill with a standby oil engine is open to visitors. This was a mill site at the time of Domesday.

Ixworth is on the site of an Augustinian priory of 1170. The cloister ranges are incorporated into the house, 'Ixworth Abbey'. Three kilometres (2 miles) to the north, the hamlet of **Ixworth Thorpe** has the church of All Saints, a delightful combination of thatched roof, wooden bell tower and a south porch in Tudor brick.

Close by is **Wyken Hall and Vineyard** where, at the heart of an ancient estate, is an Elizabethan manor house surrounded by 4hec (4acres) of lovely varied gardens, with a 3hec (7acre) vineyard adjacent. Garden and vineyard are open to the public; a 400-year old barn houses wine sales and the Leaping Hare Cafe.

Stanton Postmill at Mill Farm dates from 1751, and is remarkably intact, still producing stone ground flour. Continuing in the same direction, **Henry Watson's Potteries** at Wattisfield are carrying on an ancient pottery tradition, using local clay. This pottery, dating back for more than 180 years, has a factory shop and other visitor facilities. Turning south, via Finningham, is the **Mechanical Music Museum**, in Blacksmith Road, Cotton, where there is a large collection of music boxes, player organs and pianos, fairground organs, wurlitzers and other exhibits.

Thornham Residential Field Centre is a private country estate with visitor facilities and a network of footpaths giving 19km (12 miles) of walks through woodland, park and meadows. All-terrain wheelchairs can be hired.

Eye is a quiet little town with a small Market Place and a cross, it also has an ornate town hall and its share of antique shops. On the edge of town the Norman motte and bailey castle has medieval walls and a Victorian folly. The mound makes a superb viewpoint. At least equally important is the church of St Peter and St Paul, founded in the 12th century. The magnificent late 15th century tower rises to 35 metres (110 ft) and is decorated with flushwork. Inside, there is a good rood screen. The nearby timber framed Guildhall was restored in 1875.

Across country, to the east, **Wingfield College** was founded in 1362. Now with an 18th century neo-classical facade, the house is set in walled gardens with contemporary sculpture and a children's play area. Inside are the original medieval great hall and mixed period interiors, with changing exhibitions of paintings, prints and sculpture.

Pakenham Water Mill

Open from Good Friday to the end of September, Wednesdays, Saturdays, Sundays and Bank Holiday Mondays, 14.00 to 17.30.
☎ 01787 247179.

Wyken Hall and Vineyard

Access for wheelchairs. Open Thursday, Friday and Sunday, 10.00 to 18.00, Christmas season from mid-November, also open on Saturday. Closed from December 25th to February 9th.
☎ 01359 250287 to book for meals.

Stanton Postmill

Open on early Bank Holidays and from early July to late September, Sundays, 11.00 to 19.00.
☎ 01359 250622.

Mechanical Music Museum

Cotton. Light refreshments. Open Sundays from June to September, 14.30 to 17.30, with conducted tours.
☎ 01449 613876.

Thornham Residential Field Centre

☎ 01379 788153.
Off A140 main road about 8km (5 miles) south of Diss. *See* Walks section at end of this chapter for details of Thornham Walks through the estate.

Wingfield Old College

Follow signs on B1118 Diss to Framlingham road or B1116 Harleston to Fressingfield road. Children's play area. Crafts and gifts for sale. Cafe. Open from mid-April to late Sept, Sat, Sun and Bank Holiday Mondays, 14.00 to 18.00. ☎ 01379 384888.

South Elmham to Needham Market

To the north-east of Wingfield the road leads to an area where every village seems to be called 'Elmham' in one form or another. At South Elmham, St Peter's Brewery is based at **St Peter's Hall**, on the site of a 14th century monastery. Recently built, the brewery uses water from its own borehole and locally malted barley to produce cask conditioned ales.

South Elmham Hall lies in gently rolling countryside near St Cross South Elmham. A network of footpaths visits the ruins of an 11th century minster, a hall which was a Bishop's Palace and a herd of rare British White cattle. At Flixton, the **Norfolk and Suffolk Aviation Museum** has more than 25 historic aircraft and many other related exhibits. Museums and memorials of several individual air force units are incorporated.

A fair distance back to the south-west, the **Mid-Suffolk Light Railway Museum** is at Brockford Station, Wetheringsett. This working museum is dedicated to the former MSLR, with restoration of the station, the installation of track on part of the former route and a collection of artefacts and memorabilia.

Nearby is **Debenham**, a quiet village near the head of the River Deben, with a rising main street, some old buildings and a few shops. The **Teapot Pottery** specialises in handmade teapots of extravagant and bizarre designs. South-west of Debenham, **Stonham Barns** is described as a 'Leisure, shopping and rural pursuits complex'. It includes the **British Birds of Prey Centre**, with flying displays, Abbey Aquatics and Abbey Reptiles, nature centre, many shops, golf driving range, crazy golf, children's events and activities.

Helmingham Hall has gardens and parkland, with safari rides. The coach house and stable block are used as tearoom and shops respectively. A little way to the south-east, **Otley Hall** is a beautiful 15th century moated hall,

rich in architectural detail and history, set in 4hec (10acres) of gardens. **Baylham House Rare Breeds Farm** is located on the Roman site of Combretovium, off the B1113, 3km (2miles) east of Needham Market. Cattle, sheep and poultry are all included, with children's paddock, riverside walks and a visitor centre.

Needham Market, at the heart of a prosperous area, is basically a one street town, with Georgian houses, colour-washed cottages, craft and antique shops. The church presses hard against the side of the street, leaving no space for churchyard or bell tower. A projecting porch carries what looks like an apology for a spire and the cement rendering of the clerestory is also odd. Visitors should, however, go inside to see an unusual and very fine double hammerbeam roof.

On the eastern edge of town, Needham Lake is a pleasant local facility for anglers and model boat enthusiasts, with picnic tables and children's play area. **Alder Carr Farm**, on the northern fringe of Needham Market, has traditional Suffolk barns housing craft workshops and the sale of home grown fruits and vegetables, with a children's play area outside. The tearoom is in an attractively converted cow byre. There is a walk by the side of the River Gipping to Needham Lake.

Norfolk and Suffolk Aviation Museum

Homersfield Road, Flixton. Open from Easter to October, Sundays and Bank Holidays, 10.00 to 17.00. Summer school holidays, Tuesday, Wednesday and Thursday, 10.00 to 17.00.
☎ 01986 896644.

Mid-Suffolk Light Railway

Wetheringsett, off A140 Diss to Needham Market road. Open mid-April to late Sept, Sundays and Bank Holiday Mondays, 11.00 to 17.00.
☎ 01449 766899.

Teapot Pottery

Debenham. Light refreshments. Open Monday to Friday, 09.00 to 17.30, Saturdays and Bank Holidays, 10.30 to 16.30, Sundays (Easter to Christmas), 14.00 to 17.00.
☎ 01728 860475.

Stonham Barns

South-west of Debenham, on the south side of the main A1120. Facilities for the disabled. Restaurant. Open daily from April to October, 09.30 to 17.30. November to March, 09.30 to 16.30.

Closed Christmas Day and Boxing Day.
☎ 01449 711755.

Helmingham Hall

Tea shop and gift shop. Open from late April to early September, 14.00 to 18.00.
☎ 01473 890363.

Otley Hall

Open Bank Holiday Sundays and Mondays, 12.30 to 18.00. Gardens from mid-April to late September, Wednesdays, 14.00 to 17.00.
☎ 01473 890264.

Baylham House Rare Breeds Farm

Picnic area. Open daily from the beginning of April to the beginning of October and October half-term. Closed on Mondays other than Bank Holidays.
☎ 01473 830264.

Alder Carr Farm

Needham Market. Tearoom. Fruit and vegetable sales. Different facilities open at varying times, for example the tearoom is open from Easter to Christmas, Tuesday to Sunday, 10.00 to 17.00.
☎ 01449 720820.

Stowmarket to Lavenham

Quite large by Suffolk standards, **Stowmarket**, is the principal town of rural south-east Suffolk. The market place is central, with adjacent shopping streets, generally businesslike rather than pretty and there are peripheral industrial and commercial areas.

The huge flint church has a clerestory roof and a tower with a rather odd spire. Much the most important place for visitors is the **Museum of East Anglian Life**, 70 acres in extent, driving a wedge through the built up area to its entrance right in the town centre. A substantial number of farm buildings have been converted to provide accommodation for a wide ranging collection of many aspects of East Anglian life, together with rare breeds of farm animals. There are also workshops, re-erected buildings such as a watermill and a chapel. The Boby building has an engineering display and Bioscope film show. The adjacent Abbotts Hall, privately owned, is on the site of a former monastic building.

Woolpit is just off the beaten track, a quiet village with a few shops and a flint and stone clerestoried church with a steeple no less than 43m (140ft) in height. The central feature of the village is a roofed over pump. From the 17th century until comparatively recent times distinctive off-white bricks have been made locally and are to be seen in the vernacular buildings; don't miss the gable wall of a cottage beside the churchyard. Other features

Local white bricks create a mellow appearance on this cottage at Woolpit

are the 400-year old **Swan Inn** and the **Woolpit Museum** in the Village Institute, where there are permanent displays of 17th century farm buildings and of local brickmaking, coupled with changing displays of life in a Suffolk village.

Quite a few miles to the south of Woolpit, are the pleasant villages of **Bildeston**, with clock tower, **Chelsworth**, with charming houses, **Monks Eleigh**, clinging to the side of the tiny River Brett and **Brent Eleigh**, which has the interesting church of St Mary, with painted reredos, 13th century rood screen and wall paintings discovered as recently as 1961. Four kilometres (2.5 miles) to the south along minor roads, the charming little 13th century **St James Chapel** at Lindsey has a thatched roof and flint walls with lancet windows. Once a chantry attached to a long gone castle, the building was used for centuries for agricultural purposes until restoration took place in 1930.

Nearby is **Kersey**, the epitome of the Suffolk village for many people, strung across a valley, with the street rising each way from the watersplash of the ford over the stream in the middle. Painted weavers' cottages stand shoulder to shoulder with lovely old inns such as the Bell. The way to the church rises past **Kersey Pottery**, famous for the distinctive 'Kersey Ware'. Fifteenth century St Mary's Church, like so many

others, was built on the proceeds of the local wool trade. Noteworthy are the hammerbeam roof, painted panels from a 15th century screen, and the roof of the south porch.

Nearby **Hadleigh** is a busy market (Friday and Saturday) town now, happily, by-passed by the main road, leaving the wide main street comparatively quiet. Despite centuries of well varied building, with colour wash and pargetting, overall, Hadleigh is not the prettiest town in Suffolk. In Church Square, however, the long church is accompanied by a fine 15th century timber framed former guildhall and a most unusual tall Elizabethan (1495) building with towers, a gateway of great extravagance for an intended new rectory.

To the south-west is **Stoke by Nayland**, thanks to Constable a name universally famous, a village set high above the valley of that most Constable of rivers, the Stour. It follows naturally that Stoke is a pretty village, graced with the fine church of St Mary the Virgin which, perched on the edge of its hill, is visible for miles. The light and airy church is accompanied by a group of timber-framed buildings which include a former guildhall, maltings and almshouses.

Lower lying and larger than its neighbour, **Nayland** has a truly wonderful array of cottages, colour washed and timber framed, some with overhanging

Museum of East Anglian Life

Stowmarket. Restaurant and gift shop. Open from early April to the beginning of November, Monday to Saturday, 10.00 to 17.00; Sunday, 11.00 to 17.00.
☎ 01449 612229.

Woolpit and District Museum

Open from late March to late September, Saturdays, Sundays and Bank Holiday Mondays, 14.30 to 17.00.
☎ 01359 240822.

Gainsborough's House

Sudbury. Wheelchair access limited to ground floor. Open from Tuesday to Saturday, 10.00 to 17.00, Sundays and Bank Holiday Mondays, 14.00 to 17.00. Closes at 16.00, November to March. Closed Mondays, Good Friday and between Christmas and New Year.
☎ 01787 372958.

River Stour Trips

Sudbury. Operational on Sundays from Easter to early October.
☎ 01787 211507.

Melford Hall

National Trust. Open on Saturdays, Sundays and Bank Holiday Mondays from April to October, 14.00 to 17.30.
☎ 01787 880286.

Kentwell Hall

Open from early March to October, with complicated variations in the days and hours, generally from 12.00, daily in high season.
☎ 01787 310207.

Lavenham Guildhall

National Trust. Tearoom and shop. Open daily from late March to the beginning of November (tearoom more restricted), 11.00 to 17.00.
☎ 01787 247646.

Little Hall

Lavenham. Open Wednesday, Thursday, Saturday and Sunday, 14.00 to 17.30, Bank Holidays, 11.00 to 17.30.
☎ 01787 247179.

upper floors. The overall effect is so harmonious that the odd ordinary brick building looks embarrassingly out of place. The church has a painting by Constable, *The Last Supper* behind the altar, a rare example of his religious work. The arch under the tower is Norman. Not far from the church look out for an unusual milestone obelisk by the side of the street.

Sudbury –
Born Gainsborough

To the north-west, via Leavenheath, lies **Sudbury** in the broad valley of the Stour, another of the modest sized market (Thursday and Saturday) towns of Suffolk, with a history of the weaving industry and as a river port. At its heart is the redundant church of St Peter, facing down Market Hill, the main street, well provided with shopping and refreshment opportunities. Outside the church stands a statue of the great painter, Thomas Gainsborough, born and bred a Sudbury man. The River Stour is still sufficiently navigable to permit local boat trips.

Gainsborough's birthplace is at 46, Gainsborough Street, in the town centre (see page 167).

The Quay Theatre offers quality productions by visiting companies.

Long Melford lies to the north of Sudbury, a truly long village with a spacious green at the north end, rich in antique and other specialist shops, inns and restaurants. Above the green, the church of the Holy Trinity, one of the finest in this county of fine churches, has a clerestory roof, massive tower and 20th century 'flushwork' flint decoration. Opposite is the 'hospital', a remarkable Elizabethan building of 1573.

Melford Hall (National Trust) is a brick-built stately home of modest size, with tiled roof and splendid chimneys. At the front is a long ha-ha; at the rear are small gardens and an extravagant gazebo. The interiors are 18th century and Regency.

Ha-ha

The name derives from your expression of surprise on meeting it – a ha-ha is a boundary to a garden or park, hidden or sunken in such a way as to not to interrupt the view.

A ha-ha was an essential ingredient in the great landscaped gardens so fashionable in the 18th century. Wealthy landowners were not satisfied with building just a mansion, they wanted to shape the whole landscape that surrounded it, with romantic vistas and sweeping views, all carefully planned and planted by landscape gardeners such as the famous 'Capability' Brown.

Kentwell Hall near Long Melford, a 16th century moated mansion of mellow brickwork, with main rooms and service areas equipped in the style of that century. The gardens and adjacent woodland are extensive; there is also a farm with rare breeds of farm animals. Events include recreations of Tudor life.

• Thomas Gainsborough •

Thomas Gainsborough, arguably England's finest portrait painter, was born in 1727 at 46 Sepulchre Street, Sudbury, (the street was renamed 'Gainsborough Street' at the end of 19th century). His father was a dealer and a weaver of fine worstead cloth until bankruptcy in 1733. He then became a postmaster, in which occupation he was succeeded by his widow after his death in 1748.

Gainsborough was educated at Sudbury Grammar School, before moving to London in about 1740, marrying in 1746 and returning to Sudbury in 1749, soon producing two daughters. In 1752 he and his family moved to live at 41, Lower Brook Street, Ipswich.

Throughout this time he was painting both portraits and landscapes. In 1758 he visited Bath, so enjoying the cosmopolitan ambience that in 1759 he went to live there, in 1768 becoming a founder member of the Royal Academy. In 1774, his final move was to London, his fame now being such that from 1776, he painted the Royal Family. He died in 1788 and is buried at Kew.

Fortunately, the house of his birth has been preserved as a permanent memorial to this fine artist and his work. The house was already old when the Gainsboroughs moved in, being converted from two smaller houses dating from about 1520. His work may be divided naturally into phases corresponding with the three main periods of his life, Suffolk, Bath and London. All are well represented at Gainsborough House.

Although Gainsborough's fame lies mainly as a portrait painter, ironically it is said that he preferred painting landscapes. The national memorial to Gainsborough is the statue erected in 1913 at the top of Market Hill in his native Sudbury.

Thanks to the wool trade, **Lavenham** was once one of the richest towns in England; it is now deservedly acclaimed for the beauty and harmony of its generous array of timber framed and colour washed buildings.

The surprisingly hilly main street is richly provided with houses, shops and inns.

Typical is the Swan Hotel, an amalgam of three 14th and 15th century cottages, becoming an inn in the 17th century. Market Place, behind the main street, has a cross of 1501, the former guildhall, housing a local history exhibition, and the 'Little Hall' of the 1390s, also open to visitors. Pride of place must go to the parish church of St Peter and St Paul, another glorious clerestoried building with a massive 43m(141ft) tower, almost cathedral-like in its proportions.

An audio tour of Lavenham is available from the Pharmacy at 99, High Street.

Giffords Hall to Ickworth House

To the west, **Giffords Hall** near Hartest has a 13hec (33acres) estate with vines, winery and rare breeds of sheep and pigs, a rose garden, wild flower meadows and a small apiary.

Cavendish lies to the southwest, a pretty village with a huge green flanked by an inn and pink-washed thatched cottages in front of the church, a scene which most photographers find irresistible. The only street has cottages, shops, and antiques. The Sue Ryder Home has the headquarters of the Sue Ryder Foundation, including a museum and restaurant and coffee shop.

Clare is a pleasant town with a small market place called Market Hill and a great Gothic wool church, St Peter and St Paul. The town centre has many traditional colour-washed buildings and the 15th century 'Ancient House', a former priest's house with extravagant pargetting.

The 10hec (25acres) **Clare Country Park** by the River Stour is centred on the old railway station, a former goods shed now serving as a visitor centre. The park includes a steep mound which is the motte of Clare Castle; a path leads to the scant remains of the medieval stonework at the top. Also within the park are 13th century Clare Priory, with its church and cloister ruins, 14th century Friars House and Cellarers Hall and Chapel. Today the latter is run by Augustinian Friars as a retreat for Pilgrims. 'Antiques World' occupies a converted warehouse by the entrance to the park.

Boyton Vineyard, Hill Farm, Boyton End, Stoke by Clare, provides tours, talks and wine tasting in the gardens of a listed period farmhouse.

Haverhill is a busy commercial and industrial centre. The Haverhill and District Local History Centre, with a large collection of local items and photographs, is in the town hall, on High Street. Heading back towards Bury St Edmunds, local breeds such as Suffolk sheep, Red Poll cattle and Suffolk Punch horses can be visited at a working farm based on the 1940-50 period, **Rede Hall Farm Park**. There is also a museum, farm walks and visitor facilities.

Ickworth House is a very unusual house, basically a huge rotunda of 18th century Italian style. There are paintings by Titian and Velasquez, silver and furniture collections. Outside are an Italian garden, terrace walk, deer enclosure, vineyard, children's play area, waymarked walks, restaurant and shop.

Giffords Hall

Hartest. Open daily from mid-April to the end of October, 11.00 to 18.00.
☎ 01284 830464.

Sue Ryder Home

Cavendish. Coffee shop. Open daily, 10.00 to 17.30. Closed on Christmas Day.
☎ 01787 280252.

Clare Castle Country Park

Open all year, daily, 08.00 to dusk. Visitor centre open daily from 10.00 to 17.00 during the summer.
☎ 01787 277491.

Boyton Vineyard

Stoke by Clare. Open daily from the beginning of April to the end of October, 10.30 to 18.00.
☎ 01440 761893.

Haverhill and District Local History Centre

Open all year, Tuesday, 19.00 to 21.00; Wednesday and Thursday, 14.00 to 16.00; Friday, 14.00 to 16.00 and 19.00 to 21.00; Saturday, 10.30 to 15.30.
☎ 01440 714962.

Rede Hall Farm Park

Approximately 10km (6 miles) south-west of Bury St Edmunds on the A143 (do not go to village of Rede). Facilities for the disabled. Cafeteria, picnic area, play area and gift shop. Open from the beginning of April to the end of Sept, 10.00 to 17.30.
☎ 01284 850695.

Ickworth House

National Trust. Open from late March to the beginning of November, 07.00 to 19.00 (park), 10.00 to 17.00 (gardens), 13.00 to 17.00 (house). Closed on Mondays (except Bank Holidays) and Thursdays.
☎ 01284 735270.

Cycle Hire

Long Melford Cycle Store

Hall Street.
☎ 01787 881810.

Norfolk and Suffolk Cycle Centre

Hamilton Road, Sudbury.
☎ 01787 310940.

Walks: Bury St Edmunds & Inland Suffolk

The **Stour Valley Path** is a 96km (60 miles) regional route from Newmarket to the Stour estuary at Cattawade.

The **Lark Valley Path** is a 21km (13 mile) path connecting Mildenhall and Bury St Edmunds, including riverside, woodland, heathland and parkland.

The short, 4km (2.5 miles) **Railway Walk** along the trackbed of a former railway line is from Hadleigh to Raydon.

Lavenham, Melford and Valley Railway Walks Three walks, none more than 6km (4 miles) in length, based on Sudbury, Long Melford and Lavenham, making a good deal of use of a former railway line.

Thornham Walks offer 19km (12 miles) of paths through Thornham Estate parkland, woodland and meadows, the home of the Henniker family. All-terrain wheelchairs available. Tearooms and picnic areas. Guided walks available. ☎ 01379 788345.

South Elmham Hall Farm Walks St Cross South Elmham. Short strolls or longer walks through a historic landscape.
☎ 01986 782526.

The **Eye Circular Walk** is a 5km (3 mile) circuit of the countryside around Eye, including the Dove Valley.
☎ 01379 788008 for free leaflet.

 Cycle Rides: Bury St Edmunds & Inland Suffolk

Undulating inland Suffolk is lovely cycling country; visitors will need little guidance on finding peaceful minor roads linking the villages and other attractions. One suggestion for a 32km (20 mile) ride is the **Godric Way**, starting in Bungay and following a scenic route around the Waveney valley. The gatehouse to Mettingham Castle and the 'Saints' villages are highlights. Leaflet from Bungay (Chamber of Commerce) or Beccles Tourist Information Centres.

Hotels

Bury St Edmunds

The Abbey Hotel
Southgate Street
☎ 01284 762020 Fax 724770

The Angel Hotel
☎ 01284 753926 Fax 750092

The Butterfly Hotel
A14 Bury East exit, 70 rooms
☎ 01284 760884 Fax 755476

The Grange Hotel
Thurston
☎ 01359 231260 Fax 231260

Twelve Angel Hill
☎ 01284 704088 Fax 725549

Lavenham

The Swan Hotel
☎ 01787 247477 Fax 248286

The Angel Hotel
☎ 01787 247388 Fax 248344

The Great House
☎ 01787 247431 Fax 248007

Long Melford

The Bull
☎ 01787 378494 Fax 880307

Sudbury

The Old Bull Hotel
☎ 01787 374120 Fax 379044

Stoke-by Nayland

The Angel Inn
☎ 01206 263245 Fax 263373

Left: An "Old Age" Traveller in Kersey Below: The ancient Nutshell Inn, Bury St Edmunds

Guest Houses and B&B

Bury St Edmunds

Avery House
2 Newmarket Road
☎ 01284 755484

Dunston Guest House
Springfield Road
☎ 01284 767981

Stoke by Nayland

Thorington Hall
17th century house
☎ 01206 337329

Hartest

Pear Tree Farm
Hartest, 8 miles from
Bury St Edmunds
☎ 01284 830217

Self-catering

Nr Hadleigh

**Stable Cottage
and the Granary**
Chattisham
☎ and Fax 01473 652210

Nr Stowmarket

Barn Cottages
5 properties at Stonham
Aspal ☎ 01449 711229

Kimberley Cottage
Moats Tye, 2 properties
☎ and Fax 01449 677766

Nayland

Gladwins Farm
Harper's Hill, 7 cottages
☎ 01206 262261 Fax 263001

Caravan and Camping Sites

Mildenhall

Caravan Club Site
(no toilet facilities)
☎ 01638 713089

Nr Bury St Edmunds

The Dell
Thurston
☎ 01359 270121

Eating Out

Long Melford

Countrymen Wine Bar
☎ 01787 312356

Sudbury

The Red Onion Bistro
☎ 01787 376777

Lavenham

The Guildhall Tearoom
(National Trust)
☎ 01787 247646

Public Transport

Trains

Just two railway lines provide passenger services through inland Suffolk: **1. Ipswich** to **Stowmarket** and **Bury St Edmunds**, then branching to **Newmarket**, **Cambridge** and **London** in one direction and **Ely**, **Peterborough**, the Midlands and the North in the other direction. Intermediate stations are at **Needham Market**, **Elmswell**, and **Thurston**. **2. Sudbury** to a junction with the main **Colchester** to **Chelmsford** and **London** line at **Marks Tey**. Intermediate stations are at **Bures** and **Wakes Colne**.

Buses

Bus services are more widespread; as in previous chapters, space does not allow listing. Visitors should not forget the advantages of the 'Sunday Rover' ticket allowing Sunday travel all over East Anglia, including many of the places and visitor attractions in inland Suffolk. Discounts for entry to visitor attractions are given in many cases.

Events: Bury St Edmunds & Inland Suffolk

Bury St Edmunds Festival
Mid-May.

South Suffolk Agricultural Show
Ingham, near Bury St Edmunds. Mid-May.

Hadleigh Show
Holbecks Park.
Mid-May.

Annual Re-creation of Tudor Life
Kentwell Hall, Long Melford.
Mid-June/early July.

Woolpit Festival
Late June.

Haverhill Show
Early July.

'Last Night of the Proms'
Ickworth House
Bury St Edmunds.
Mid-July.

Thurlow Steam Rally and Show
Haverhill showground.
Early August.

Eye Show
Eye showground
Late August.

COLCHESTER & NORTH ESSEX

Maldon

At the head of the Blackwater Estuary, Maldon is very much at the southern extremity of the territory in this book. It is included for two reasons: first, because without straying too far from the core area it rounds off a great sweep of Suffolk and Essex river estuaries and their sailing centres and, second, because it is an attractive place for visitors.

The town's history goes back to well before the Norman Conquest. At the fierce and prolonged Battle of Maldon in AD991 an invading force of Vikings defeated the troops of the local Anglo-Saxon earl. A Royal Charter is dated 1171, and by the

18th century Maldon was the second largest town in Essex. Its prosperity was assisted by a busy barge trade to and from London. In 1797 a canal was dug, by-passing the section of river in the town centre, in order to facilitate waterborne trade to and from

Above: The River Stour at Flatford Mill

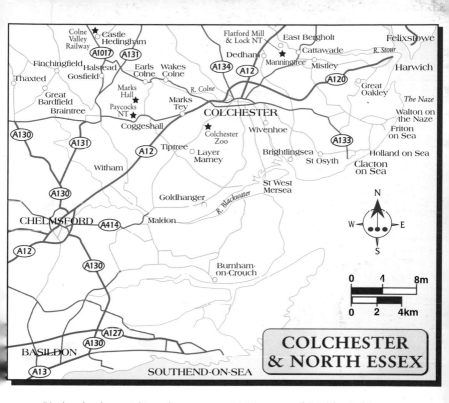

COLCHESTER
& NORTH ESSEX

Chelmsford, avoiding the payment of heavy dues to Maldon. At the Hythe (quay) are moored several of the old sailing barges.

From the area of the quay the long High Street climbs steadily to the grouping of old buildings which forms the nucleus of the town, where the 13th century church of All Saints has the only triangular church tower in England. Close by is the **Moot Hall** of about 1440, used since the late 16th century as council offices and courthouse. It now houses the Maldon Millen Embroidery, more than 12 metres (42ft) in length, in seven panels, depicting 1000 years of Maldon's history. Eighty-six women worked on this embroidery for three and a half years. The pillared balcony is 19th century.

The nave of St Peter's Church collapsed in the mid-17th century, leaving a surviving tower to which a new nave was added about 40 years later. The **Plume Library**, containing over 6000 volumes, many of them of the 16th and 17th centuries, is on the first floor of the former church.

Most of the shops are around this central area and along High Street. Markets are held on Thursday and Saturday.

Returning to the area of the quay, to the right is 12th century **St Mary's Church**, built of stone with brick additions, with its odd little white wooden steeple added to the squat tower in 1740, serving as a navigational aid for sailors. A little further along the waterside, **Promenade Park** is a long established recreational facility, Edwardian gardens with a marine lake, to which many other facilities such as catering stalls have been added.

By the entrance to the park, at 47, Mill Road, the **Maldon District Museum** has a wide ranging local collection.

Maldon to West Mersea

Leaving Maldon to the east, **Goldhanger** is a few kilometres along the B1026. Here, the Maldon and District Agricultural Domestic Museum in Church Street has a rather individualistic collection, including the products of Maldon ironworks and farming bygones.

Bend to the north to **Tiptree**, of jam fame. At Tiptree Museum and shop, Wilkins and Sons Ltd. have a display of how life was in the area and how the art of jam making has progressed over the years.

Continuing, a small diversion leads to **Layer Marney Tower** and **Home Farm**. The tower, dating from 1515-25, is a flamboyant Italianate structure in fine terracotta, the tallest Tudor gatehouse in the country, built by Henry, the first Lord Marney, Privy Seal to King Henry VIII. The climb to the top is rewarded by long views from the roof and interesting interiors along the way.

Linked with a visit to the tower is the Home Farm; rare breeds of animals, including Bagot goats, are kept in adjacent barns and farm walks are available. The Stables Tearoom provides refreshment and there is also a farm shop. Close by is the small church of **St Mary the Virgin**, constructed in 1520 on earlier foundations. Internal renovations of the late 19th and early 20th centuries have produced a pleasingly Italianate style. A wall painting of St Christopher was obscured in 1552 but has subsequently been uncovered.

Cutting across country to the south of Colchester leads to Abberton, with its large reservoir, and **Mersea Island**, reached by an ancient causeway across Strood Channel. The island is a great attraction for small boat sailors, largely based on the extensive quay area of **West Mersea**. The town itself is mainly residential, with a very modest shopping centre, but the old area behind and along the quay is more interesting, with fishermen's cottages, some shiplap boarded, a 14th century church, inn and the jumble of maritime activity.

Mersea Island Museum, covering local social and natural history, fishing and wild-fowling, is in High Street.

Colchester

Colchester has a good claim to be the oldest town in England and, following the establishment of an encampment on the River Colne, the first capital of Roman Britain. In the 11th century the incoming Normans built Colchester Castle, with the biggest keep in Europe, largely using stone from the Roman fortifications. The town walls are claimed to be the oldest in Britain, with the Balkerne Gate, in Balkerne Street, as the largest surviving Roman gateway in the country.

Places to Visit
From Maldon to West Mersea

Maldon District Museum

Open from May onwards, Wednesdays, 10.00 to 14.00; Saturdays, 10.00 to 16.00; Sundays 12.00 to 16.00. ☎ 01621 842688.

The Plume Library

Maldon. Open Tuesday, Wednesday and Thursday, 14.00 to 16.00; Saturday, 10.00 to 12.00. ☎ 01621 855912.

Moot Hall

Maldon. Visits by arrangement with Maldon Town Council. ☎ 01621 857373.

Maldon and District Agricultural and Domestic Museum

Goldhanger. Open from the beginning of April to the end of October, Wednesday, 14.00 to 18.00, Sunday, 10.00 to 18.00. ☎ 01621 788647.

Tiptree Museum

Wilkins and Sons Ltd. Tearoom and shop. Open from early January to the end of June, Monday to Saturday, 10.00 to 17.00. July and August, daily, 10.00 to 17.00. September to 24th December, Monday to Saturday, 10.00 to 17.00. ☎ 01621 815407.

Layer Marney Tower

Tearoom and farm shop. Open from the beginning of April to early October, 12.00 to 17.00, Bank Holidays, 1100 to 1800. ☎ 01206 330784.

Mersea Island Museum

West Mersea. Open from the beginning of May to late September, Wednesday to Sunday and Bank Holiday Mondays, 1400 to 1700. ☎ 01206 385191.

Roman rule of Colchester, and the south-east of England generally, suffered a major but temporary setback when, in AD60 the sorely provoked Boudicca, Queen of the local Iceni tribe, attacked the town, burned it to the ground and massacred the inhabitants. She went on to destroy London and St Albans before the Romans could organise the necessary forces to contain and then subjugate her rebellion.

In the Middle Ages the town prospered on cloth making and fishery, with a market charter granted by King Henry V in 1413 and a busy river port. Late in the 16th century incoming Protestant refugees from Europe gave a boost to the cloth trade. Half timbered and plastered houses in Stockwell Street were known as the 'Dutch Quarter'. In 1648, the Civil War brought a siege which lasted for 11 weeks, followed by the execution, outside the castle, of the defending commanders Sir Charles Lucas and Sir George Lisle.

Among the town's several churches, **Holy Trinity** is of Saxon origin, with the use of Roman materials and a particularly old west wall of the nave, which has a triangular headed door. The church is now used as a crafts museum. Of the former Benedictine St John's Abbey of 1096, only the 15th century gatehouse remains.

The **Castle Museum** is a major attraction, with comprehensive local displays including audio-visual dramas and full visitor facilities. Close by are the **Natural History Museum** and the **Hollytrees Museum**, both in High Street. The latter specialises in toys of previous generations. A short

Colchester

Castle Museum

Tours available. Open daily, Monday to Saturday, 10.00 to 17.00, Sunday 14.00 to 17.00 (March to November only). ☎ 01206 282931.

Natural History Museum

High Street. Open from Tuesday to Saturday, 10.00 to 17.00 (closed from 13.00 to 14.00). ☎ 01206 282931.

Hollytrees Museum

Open from Tuesday to Saturday, 10.00 to 17.00 (closed from 13.00 to 14.00). ☎ 01206 282931.

Tymperleys Clock Museum

Open from April to October, Tuesday to Saturday, 10.00 to 17.00 (closed from 13.00 to 14.00). ☎ 01206 282931.

Bourne Mill

National Trust. Open on Bank Holiday Sundays and Mondays, plus Sundays and Tuesdays in July and August, 14.00 to 17.30. ☎ 01206 572422.

Colchester Zoo

Facilities for the disabled. Refreshments at inn and other outlets. Shop. Open daily (except Christmas Day) from 09.30, last admissions at 17.30 in summer, one hour before dusk out of season.

distance away from the castle, in Trinity Street, a 15th century timber framed house has **Tymperleys Clock Museum,** a comprehensive collection of locally made 18th and 19th century clocks.

In the 19th century engineering became the most important industry and Colchester is now an attractive mixture of the old and the new, certainly the most important town in North Essex. The shopping centre is comprehensive, mingling narrow old streets with modern malls, largely pedestrianised, all close to the impressive town hall of 1902, with its melodious chiming clock.

Markets are held on Friday and Saturday. Castle Park provides a green oasis very close to the centre.

Bourne Mill, in Bourne Road, was a stone fishing lodge built in 1591 on the banks of Bourne Brook. In the 19th century it was converted to a mill for yarn spinning and, later, flour milling. The waterwheel and some machinery is now in working order, in the care of the National Trust. The Minories Art Gallery, a Georgian house close to the castle, houses an important visual arts organisation. Theatre and cinema are also well catered for by the

Mercury Theatre and the Odeon.

At Maldon Road, Stanway, to the south of the town, **Colchester Zoo** is well known for its fine collection of animals and for its breeding programme. One hundred and seventy species are housed in enclosures in a naturalistic environment. Particular features are the elephant enclosures, the discovery area and daily presentations.

Colchester railway station has services to London via Chelmsford and to Ipswich and Norwich to the north, with a branch line to Manningtree. Another branch line, direct from Colchester, serves Clacton, Walton and Frinton.

Wivenhoe to St Osyth

A little more than 6km (4 miles) down river, at the point where it is widening to become an estuary, is **Wivenhoe**, a little town with a marked maritime ambience. From the attractive nucleus of the quay, with its fishing and boatbuilding activity backed by shiplap boarded and colour-washed buildings, modern residential development has expanded the town. The rather squat church has a cupola on the tower. An old ferry across the river has been revived, operating from the quay at weekends between Easter and October, two hours either side of high tide.

The **Nottage Institute** on the quay has been the heart of maritime Wivenhoe since 1886, when it was founded to train yacht crews and sailors on the River Colne. The Institute has a museum of maritime memorabilia, displays and exhibits.

Wivenhoe has a station on the Colchester to Walton, Frinton and Clacton branch railway line.

Continuing down river via Alreford, **Brightlingsea** is another small maritime town with substantial inland development which has provided a reasonable shopping centre, laid out with trees and gardens. **Jacobes Hall** is a timber framed building of great antiquity, with 13th century origins. **Brightlingsea Museum** specialises in local maritime and social history, including the story of the former Brightlingsea branch railway line. The original heart of the town is, however, the quay area, now a major yacht sailing centre.

An inland detour via Thorrington, necessary to avoid Flag Creek, leads on to **St Osyth**, a large village set back from its quay and sailing area at the head of navigation of St Osyth Creek. Once again, the history is maritime but there are the remains of a substantial abbey of the 12th century, unfortunately without public access. Here, a very early foundation was refounded in 1161; after dissolution the remains were incorporated into a private house, 'St Osyth Priory'.

The flint, brick and stone gatehouse was built in 1475. Church Square has shops and old houses.

Clacton to Mistley

Clacton on Sea grew from a quiet village to a considerable seaside resort over a short space of time, capitalising on the classic formula of sea, sand and sunshine. The south facing long, sandy, beach was soon reinforced by the addition of pier, funfair and other amusements. The spacious tree-lined streets and good public gardens have, however, helped to maintain a greater dignity than is usual in seaside holiday resorts. There are two theatres, the Princes and the West Cliff, providing entertainment throughout the season. The pier is claimed to be the 'largest fun pier in Europe', with a funfair which includes several up to date rides.

The railway station has services along the branch line to Colchester, including through trains to London. Markets are held on Tuesday and Saturday.

Holland on Sea is a seaside suburb of Clacton, with Holland Haven Country Park, a large area for picnic and car parking with access both to the coastal footpath and to the beach.

Frinton is a quiet little holiday town behind a long stretch of sandy beach. The elegant main shopping street has been called the 'Bond Street of East Anglia'.

There is live theatre during the summer season. Amazingly, the town has been without a pub until recent proposals to change this situation, perhaps to celebrate the millennium!

In contrast, **Walton on the Naze** is a jollier place, with more of the 'fun of the fair', always more popular with holidaymakers than its neighbour. The 244m (800ft) pier has attractions which include 10-pin bowling, and the sea front gardens are colourful. Behind the town are the 'backwaters', saltings and little harbours.

The Naze (Ness – headland) is a considerable promontory, now a **National Nature Reserve** for birds, with a Nature Trail. By the car park, the Naze Tower acts as a guide for mariners. A carefully restored 100 year old former life-boat house serves as **Walton Maritime Museum**, with local maritime exhibitions, changed annually. Both towns are served by the railway line to Colchester. Thursday is market day.

A circuitous inland drive through Great Oakley is required to reach **Harwich**, on its promontory at the junction of the estuaries of the Rivers Stour and Orwell. Long a seafaring township, the town was a Naval Headquarters visited by King Charles II. The town was walled and some narrow streets and passageways still preserve something of a medieval atmosphere. At 21 King's Head Street was the home of Captain Christopher

"The Leading Lights" used in the past to guide ships into Harwich

Lifeboat Museum, at Timberfields, off Wellington Road, has the last of the historic off-shore 12m (37ft) Oakley class lifeboats and a display of local lifeboat history.

Harwich Maritime Museum, at the Low Lighthouse on The Green, has special displays relating to the Royal Navy and to commercial shipping. **The Redoubt** is a sizeable coastal defence construction a little way along the coast in the Dovercourt direction.

Other Harwich buildings of interest include the town's oldest house, on Tower Hill. Of about 1450, this building was formerly an ale house. The Guildhall dates from 1769 and the 'Electric Palace' is an early (1911) cinema. Harwich has a railway branch line connecting with the main Colchester to Ipswich line at Manningtree.

Returning towards Colchester, the **Essex Secret Bunker** at **Mistley** is an unusual attraction. The intended nuclear war headquarters for the county, both above and below ground, has been restored and equipped. On view are the giant operations room, heating and filtration plant, power station and dormitory. The site includes an exhibition gallery, shop and visitor facilities.

A little way further, **Mistley Towers** are the remains of a church of 1735, remodelled by Adam in 1776. The central portion was demolished in 1870,

Jones, master of the Pilgrim Fathers' ship, *Mayflower*.

On Harwich Green stands what is probably the only surviving treadmill crane in the world, a remarkable 17th century contraption with double tread wheel. A market is held on Fridays.

Adjoining Harwich, Dovercourt and Upper Dovercourt are a minor seaside resort and a residential and shopping area respectively. Three kilometres (2 miles) west of Harwich, on the Stour estuary, Parkeston has become a main terminal for ferry services to Holland. **Harwich**

Walton Maritime Museum

Walton on the Naze. Open from the beginning of July to the end of September, daily, 14.00 to 16.00. October, Saturday and Sunday, 14.00 to 16.00.
☎ (Tourist Infomation point) 01255 675542.

Harwich Lifeboat Museum

Open daily from the beginning of May to the end of August, 10.00 to 17.00. September, Sunday, 10.00 to 12.00 and 14.00 to 17.00.
☎ (Tourist Information Centre) 01255 506139.

Harwich Maritime Museum

Open April, Sunday, 10.00 to 12.00 and 14.00 to 17.00. Beginning of May to the end of August, daily, 10.00 to 17.00. September, Sunday, 10.00 to 12.00 and 14.00 to 17.00.
☎ 01255 503429.

Essex Secret Bunker

Mistley. Cafe, picnic site and gift shop. Open from Good Friday to the end of September, daily, 10.30 to 16.30. October, November, February, March, Saturday and Sunday, 10.30 to 16.00.
☎ 01206 392271.

Mistley Place Park

Tearooms and gift shop. Open daily, 10.00 to 18.00 (tearooms closed each Monday, other than on Bank and school Holidays).
☎ 01206 396048.

leaving just the two ornate towers. **Mistley Place Park** is an environmental and animal rescue centre, a remarkable place at which visitors mingle freely with many of the more than 2000 birds and animals, all rescued from threatened slaughter, ill-treatment and neglect. The park comprises many acres, with maze and nature trail. Tearoom, gift shop and toilets are available for visitors.

Mistley has a railway station on the branch line which connects Harwich with the main Colchester to Ipswich line at Manningtree.

Manningtree to East Bergholt

Next to Mistley, **Manningtree** is promoted as 'England's smallest town'. Formerly a thriving port, with one long street parallel with the River Stour, the town has many and varied old houses, inns and shops. Many of the Georgian facades conceal Tudor or Elizabethan houses. Much of the early wealth of the town came from the cloth trade; examples of weavers' cottages still stand in Brook Street and South Street. The artist John Constable's father owned two boatyards by the Quay.

Matthew Hopkins, notorious as the witchfinder of the 17th century, began his career at Manningtree by condemning an alleged coven of witches, later continuing his profitable (twenty shillings per witch!) activities at Colchester. He is buried at Mistley Heath. The market charter was granted in 1238; morning markets are still held each Wednesday and Saturday.

Constable Country

After Manningtree, we are well and truly into 'Constable Country', which follows close to his own river – the Stour – as far inland as Nayland. **Dedham** is a good place to start, with lovely old buildings along the High Street, both timber framed and elegant Georgian, a happy mixture. The flint church of St Mary has a massive tower; adjacent is the Dedham Centre with arts and crafts, refreshments and the **Toy Museum**. The latter has an intriguing collection.

One hundred yards along a track from the High Street, the Duchy Barn has been refurbished, now housing tourist information, with adjacent public conveniences. Beside this track, the grammar school attended by Constable is now two separate houses.

A little more than one kilometre (600 yards) south of Dedham, **Castle House** was the home of the painter Sir Alfred Munnings for 40 years, reminding us that Constable was not the only local painter. The house has a large collection, representing Munnings's life's work.

Dedham Rare Breeds Farm in Mill Lane occupies 12hec (30acres) of rolling countryside close to the village centre. Sheep, horses, cattle, pigs and poultry are all represented, with pets' corner, picnic area, country walks and refreshments. Just out of Dedham, at the point where the minor road to the north reaches the River Stour, an attractive little area has Dedham Mill (not open to the public), a waterside cafe and boat hire.

To cross the river by car for exploration of the north side, a return to Manningtree is advised, then turning left to **Flatford Mill**, part of a hamlet which also includes **Willy Lott's Cottage**. The mill, once owned by Constable's father, is now a field studies centre. Arguably, as the setting for so many of his best loved paintings, such as *The Hay Wain* and *Flatford Mill*, this grouping of buildings and river is where one is closest to Constable's heart, the one place which must be visited in order to fully appreciate the sources of his inspiration. Even better is also to walk, as he did so often, across the fields to Dedham and back. (see 'Walks' below).

Also close to Flatford Mill is 16th century Bridge Cottage, owned by the National Trust, containing tea shop, gift shop and a display about Constable, who featured the building in several of his paintings. Guided walks to the sites of several of his paintings are available during the season. Boats can be hired beside the bridge. Finally, Granary Museum, a large shiplap boarded building beside the mill has a collection of bygones. The large car park is well landscaped.

Continue to the north-west for a short distance to **East Bergholt**, a village with many large elegant houses, formerly the homes of wool merchants. In this area it is impossible to escape the influence of Constable; East Bergholt is his birthplace.

The church is an odd mixture of brick and flint. As the construction was nearing completion, the builders were believed to be running out of funds, hence the lack of a bell tower. The bells, of abnormal size, were housed in a 'cage', intended to be temporary, in the churchyard. Constable's parents are buried here. Inside is a decorated organ, a memorial to Constable's wife, Maria, and a board below a window with quotes from Constable on art, patrons and on other British painters.

East Bergholt Place Garden covers 6hec (15acres). It was laid out about 100 years ago by the great grandfather of the present owner. Many of the trees and shrubs are comparatively rare in East Anglia. Spring is the best season, when magnolias, camellias and rhododendrons are in flower, with topiary hedges and ornamental ponds adding to the overall attraction.

Places to Visit
From Manningtree to East Bergholt

Toy Museum, Art and Craft Centre
Dedham. Refreshments. Open from January to March, Tuesday, Wednesday and Friday to Sunday, 10.00 to 17.00. April to December, daily except Thursday, 10.00 to 17.00. Closed on Christmas Day, Boxing Day and New Year's Day.
☎ 01206 322666.

Castle House
Dedham (Munnings collection). Open every Sunday, Wednesday and Bank Holiday Monday from early May to

Continued on page 186...

185

March April and October, Wednesday to Sunday, 11.00 to 17.30. May to September, daily, 10.00 to 17.30.
☎ 01206 299193.

East Bergholt Place Garden

Open from the beginning of March to October, Tuesday to Sunday and Bank Holiday Mondays, 10.00 to 17.00.
☎ 01206 299224.

early October. Also Thursday and Saturday in August, 14.00 to 17.00.
☎ 01206 322127.

Dedham Vale Family Farm

Playground, picnic area, gift shop and light refreshments. Open daily from early March to the end of September, 10.30 to 17.30.
☎ 01206 323111.

Bridge Cottage

Flatford Mill (National Trust). Wheelchair and battery operated vehicle. Tearoom and shop. Open during

Above: The Toy Museum, Dedham

Below: Flatford Mill

Asked to name the painter who most beautifully depicted the English countryside as it was before the advancing tide of mechanisation shattered the rural idyll forever, the answer for most would be 'Constable'. England's greatest landscape painter was essentially an East Anglian man, finding inspiration in the gentle contours of the Stour Valley, the little towns, the villages and the nearby coast.

As we see with Wordsworth's poetry, there was then a prevailing presumption that not only was mankind living in perfect harmony with nature but was also content and even happy with the stability of a rigid social order, pre-ordained and unchanging for the peasants, living in what would now be regarded as squalor, doffing their caps as required.

To be fair to Constable it is evident that he was less interested in this sentimentalisation of rural humanity than some of his lesser contemporaries; to him the glory of the landscape itself was paramount.

Constable was born on 11th June 1776 at East Bergholt, his parents being Golding and Ann Constable. The house in which he was born has gone, marked only by a plaque on the fence of the house 'Constables'. A little further up, on the other side of the road, is a tiny cottage, now a private house, which he used as a studio. As the owner of mills, including Flatford, and boatyards at Manningtree, his parents were comfortably off and for a short time he attended a boarding school in Lavenham. He was not happy at this school and most of his education was at the grammar school in Dedham, walking across the fields and crossing the Stour each day between that village and East Bergholt. The school has since been converted into two houses.

Although Constable travelled a good deal, his heart never left his beloved Essex and Suffolk countryside, as paintings such as *The Haywain*, *Flatford Mill* and *Willy Lott's Cottage* demonstrate.

Constable's parents are buried at East Bergholt Church; inside the church is a stained glass memorial window to him and a memorial to Maria, his wife. St James Church at Nayland has a rare Constable religious painting behind the altar – Christ blessing the bread and the wine. After achieving great fame comparatively late in life, Constable died in 1837.

Coggeshall to Thaxted

The itinerary continues to the west of Colchester, best passed by the use of the A12 main road, forking right on to the A120, close to Marks Tey. The quaintly named **St James the Less** at Little Tey is a small church signposted to the right one kilometre (600 yards) after passing Marks Tey. Described by English Heritage as 'a tiny church of national importance', this Norman church has recently restored wall paintings of the 13th century. It has to be said that, although the historic importance of the paintings cannot de denied, the colours are very faint.

From Little Tey, head north via Great Tey to Chappel and Wakes Colne for the **East Anglian Railway Museum**, a comparatively rare combination of an operational railway station (on the Sudbury to Marks Tey branch line) and a railway preservation centre. The latter occupies 1.6hec (4 acres); on the near side of the railway line, in the original station buildings, is a visitor centre with displays of local railway history, whilst across the tracks are collections of locomotives, other rolling stock and relics such as signal boxes, engineering and restoration workshops. Occasional 'steam days' are held.

At the near end of **Earls Colne** a little wayside curiosity is a 'chol-era pump' provided in 1853 to supply clean, wholesome, water. The inscription shows distinct linguistic oddity in that the well was 'digged' and the intention was to 'provoke' cleanliness.

Turn to the south on the B1024 towards Coggeshall, turning right to reach the **Marks Hall Estate**. This extensive privately owned area has a visitor centre in a restored 15th century barn, surrounded by rolling countryside including 300 acres of woodland, arboretum, ornamental lakes and a 17th century walled garden under restoration. Several walks on good tracks are recommended.

Coggeshall lies a little way to the south, a busy small market (Thursday) town despite being by-passed. There are many good old buildings and a shiplap boarded clock tower of 1787, restored in the late 19th century, but as a whole the town doesn't pose a threat to Lavenham. The star feature is **Paycocke's**, an early 16th century family house now owned by the National Trust.

In conjunction with Paycocke's, the Trust also owns and manages Grange Barn, allegedly the oldest surviving timber-framed barn in Europe. Although it was a ruin as recently as 1982, 60 per cent of the main timbers are original. The display includes the history of the nearby priory. Grange Barn is the recommended car parking place for visitors to Paycocke's.

Coggeshall Priory was founded by King Stephen in 1140; the ruins are not open to the public.

Halstead is a modest market (Tuesday, Friday and Saturday) and former weaving town on the River Colne, with a charter granted by King Henry III in 1256. The main thoroughfare, Head Street/High Street, slopes down to the river, where a left turn leads to the **Tourist Information Centre** and to Townsford Mill, now an antiques centre. There is a river walk. Shops, inns and restaurants are plentiful, with a small modern precinct and the Empire cinema.

Castle Hedingham derives its name from the adjacent castle, sitting high above on its wonderful hilltop site, dominating the Colne Valley. The Norman keep was built by the de Veres, Earls of Oxford and is approached over a shapely Tudor bridge. The castle is 34 metres (110ft) high, with walls nearly four metres (12ft) thick. Kings Henry VII and VIII and Queen Elizabeth I were all visitors and the castle was besieged by King John.

The domestic Norman interior is sumptuous; the banqueting hall, with minstrels' gallery, having the finest Norman arch in England. The extensive grounds include a lake, valley and woodland walks. The castle is in the care of English Heritage and has the usual visitor facilities.

The former woollen town has a market charter granted by King John in the 13th century. Although the market is long gone, a striking village remains, with fine Georgian wool merchants' houses in King Street and Queen Street. The clustering of houses in the narrow streets is unfailingly photogenic. The church of St Nicholas has parts as old as the castle subsumed into a generally Tudor structure, the tower being renovated in 1616. A circular Norman 'wheel' window over the altar is one of only five such windows in the country.

Strung along the adjacent main road, Sible Hedingham provides for the business and shopping requirements of the Hedinghams.

On the site of a defunct railway line nearby, the **Colne Valley Railway** has been painstakingly built up from nothing by dedicated enthusiasts into an authentic rural Suffolk station, with a running track of more than one kilometre and numerous other railway attractions. The locomotives include a 'Bulleid' Pacific of the former Southern Railway and there is plenty of other rolling stock. From March to October, and again before Christmas, a service of trains is operated, frequent in high season and during school holidays. Meals in a Pullman coach, special events days and driver training are all on offer.

Finchingfield is undoubtedly a showpiece village, posing itself shamelessly to view as it climbs the hillside above its stream and duck pond. White-painted

Paycocke's House

Built by wool merchant John Paycocke for his son Thomas on the latter's marriage, the opulent decoration and the close spacing of the expensive oak upright structural members are indications of considerable wealth. Many alterations and enlargements can be traced, giving a fascinating insight into the fashions prevailing at particular times over the centuries.

In the late 18th century it was converted into tenements, a fairly reliable sign of decline. So decrepit was it that in 1885 the house came close to demolition, but was renovated in 1905. The facade is the great and obvious glory, much changed, particularly in 1905, but nevertheless still having the original main timbers, much of the brick nogging and other features.

Inside, five rooms are open to the public, one having a permanent display of the lace for which Coggeshall became famous early in the 19th century, following the arrival of skilled French immigrants. The house is complemented by attractive gardens at the rear, from which the rear extensions, older than the front part of the house, may be appreciated.

cottages, with church above, and a windmill away to the left all add to the charm of this place of broad greens, inns and tearooms. Part way up the hill, the 15th century guildhall serves as a local museum, with Roman remains among its collection. The adjacent arch through the almshouses leads to the churchyard, where the church of St John the Baptist has a Norman tower and a Georgian style bellcote. It is no surprise to find that antique shops predominate in this popular village. Duck End postmill is a small, simple, 18th century windmill. A little way to the south,

Great Bardfield has a 17th century village lock-up, Bardfield Cage, in Bridge Street.

Thaxted, with its claim to '900 years of history' is yet another former wool town. Town Street climbs up to the celebrated 15th century **Guildhall of the Cutlers** and a tall-spired church. The street is lined with colour-washed cottages and shops, with the odd inn and teashop. Whilst he was organist at the parish church, the composer Gustave Holst lived from 1917-25 at a house in Town Street which was 'modernised' in the 18th century, when many of the old houses were changed to reflect the then current popularity of the Georgian style, perhaps an early example of keeping up with the Jones's!

The cobbled street, Stoney Lane, beside the guildhall has **Dick Turpin's Cottage** on the left, believed to be a one-time home of the notorious highwayman and the Guildhall itself has a small local history museum. **John Webb's Windmill** of 1804 is behind the church, with intact machinery and a rural museum. Nearby is the old, thatched Chantry row of almshouses. Clarence House, at the top of the town, is a fine example of Queen Anne architecture. It is worth mentioning that the public conveniences are well concealed behind Clarence House.

Markets are held each Friday as they have been for several centuries.

Places to Visit
From Coggeshall to Thaxted

St James the Less

Little Tey. Open all year round, Thursday, Friday, Saturday, Sunday and Bank Holidays, 09.30 to dusk.
☎ 01206 210396.

East Anglian Railway Museum

Wakes Colne. Toilets for the disabled, book shop, picnic area. Open frequently throughout the season and before Christmas.
☎ 01206 242524 for details.

Paycocke's House

National Trust.
Coggeshall. Open from late March to mid-October, Tuesday, Thursday, Sunday and Bank Holiday Mondays, 14.00 to 17.30.
☎ 01376 561305.

Grange Barn

National Trust.
Coggeshall. Open from late March to mid-October, Tuesday, Thursday, Sunday and Bank Holiday Mondays, 13.00 to 17.00. ☎ as above.

Gosfield Lake Resort

Cafes, picnic areas and children's play area. Usually open but ☎ 01787 475043 for details.

Hedingham Castle

English Heritage.
Gift shop and tearoom.
Open daily from early April until the end of September, 10.00 to 17.00.
☎ 01787 460261.

Continued on page 192...

Places to Visit
From Coggeshall to Thaxted

Colne Valley Railway

Castle Hedingham. Refreshments and gift shop. Open for static inspection most days, 10.00 to 17.00 (or dusk if earlier). Trains run in accordance with a detailed timetable. Obtain a copy or ☎ 01787 461174.

Finchingfield Guildhall

Open from late March to late September, Sunday and Bank Holiday Mondays, 14.30 to 17.30. ☎ 01371 810456.

Duck End Postmill

Finchingfield. Open from mid-April to mid-September, third Sunday of each month, 14.00 to 17.00. ☎ 01621 828162.

Bardfield Cage

Bardfield. Open from late March to late September, Saturday, Sunday and Bank Holiday Mondays, 14.00 to 18.00.

Thaxted Guildhall

Open from late March to the end of September, Saturday, Sunday and Bank Holiday Mondays, 14.00 to 18.00. ☎ 01371 831339.

John Webb's Windmill

Mill Row, Thaxted. Open from the beginning of May to late September, Saturday, Sunday and Bank Holiday Mondays, 14.00 to 18.00. ☎ 01371 830285.

Walks: Colchester & North Essex

 1 **Monks Hall Estate**, north of Coggeshall. Waymarked trails in woodland and rolling countryside, up to about 5km (3 miles) in length.

 2 **Layer Marney Tower**, near Tiptree. Short and easy walks around adjacent farmland.

 3 Dedham

A local leaflet, obtainable at the Tourist Information Centre, has two circular walks, set out in full detail. Both meander through the attractive countryside to the west, south and east of the village. The longer, 10km (6 miles), walk heads to the west to pass by Dalethorpe and the Dedham Vale Hotel, then turns south towards Monks Lane Farm, May's Barn, The Orchard, Winterflood House, Hill Farm and Stour House. The shorter route, 5km (3 miles) leaves the village past the Duchy Barn, then by Weavers'

Cottages and Brook Farm to join the longer route at the Orchard. At East Lane, this route turns left to leave the longer walk, returning behind East House to Weavers Cottages and Dedham.

↑4 Flatford Mill and Dedham 4.5km (under 3 miles).

Apart from being a very attractive short walk in its own right, this highly recommended circuit has a guaranteed appeal to anyone (which must mean most people) with even a passing interest in Constable and the landscape which so inspired him and which he, in turn, has immortalised.

Park at the large car park close to Flatford Mill and walk down the path to the River Stour. Pass Bridge House, with its various facilities, and cross over the river bridge. Turn right to follow a signpost 'Public Footpath, Dedham'.

The good, level, path follows the willow-lined river bank for some distance; go over a stile and continue to Fen Bridge. Don't cross, but bear left here, following another 'Dedham' signpost.

After crossing a tiny bridge the tower of Dedham Church, which features in more than one of Constable's paintings, comes into view. The path is always easy to follow as it passes part of the Dedham Vale Family Farm. Bear a little to the left along the farm access road to reach the public road at one end of Dedham village.

Turn right to pass the craft centre and then right again. opposite the church, into Mill Lane. Walk past the village car park, as far as the river. Between the restored but private mill complex and the river, turn left to reach Dedham Lock. Go into the adjacent meadow and turn right to return to the public road. To the right are a waterside tea garden and boats for hire.

Turn left at the public road, then right in a few metres at a kissing gate, signposted 'E. Bergholt, Flatford'. In less than 400m (0.25 mile) the track bends to the left, away from the river, to reach a waymarked kissing gate. So far the route has been across the Stour water meadows.

After the gate the path is between outgrown hedges, soon joining a more important track. Unless a return partly along the outward route is desired, turn left here for East Bergholt. Cross a bridge over rather stagnant water to a junction in 50m (45 yards). Go ahead over a stile with a 'Public Footpath' sign to rise gently over grass up the valley side.

Reach a surfaced lane and turn right along the roadside foot-path, behind the hedge on the far side. Rejoin the lane, rising a little to a junction. Turn right into the car park.

Continued on page 194...

Coninued...

↑5 **The Wivenhoe Trail** is a cycle way and footpath beside the
•••• River Colne, starting at Wivenhoe railway station and
continuing beside Wivenhoe Woods and along the river bank to
Colchester Hythe (quay). Accessible for wheelchairs and vehicles
for disabled people; a radar key will open the gate.

↑6 **Highwoods Country Park**, Colchester. Although fringed by the
•••• Colchester urban area, Highwoods has more than 121hec
(300acres) of woodland, grassland, farm and wetland, with an
extensive network of footpaths providing circular walks of up to
5km (3 miles) in length.

Cycle Rides: Colchester & North Essex

The quiet lanes of Constable Country, never far from the River
Stour, are ideal for gentle cycling.
   The Wivenhoe Trail, mentioned under 'Walks' is also a cycle way.

CYCLE HIRE

Gosfield Lake Resort
Mountain Bike Trekking Centre.
☎ 01787 475043.

Bicycle Breaks
Colchester. In addition to
standard cycle hire, complete
holiday arrangements can be
made. ☎ 01206 868254.

Dedham Vale Cycle Hire
Near Colchester.
☎ 0370 596604.

The Spinning Wheel
West Mersea.
☎ 01206 384013.

Buckley-Saxon
Castle Hedingham.
☎ 01787 461755.

East Essex Cycles
Clacton on Sea.
☎ 01255 434490.

EXCURSION TO BRAINTREE

From this southernmost part of East Anglia, the first suggestion is a short excursion to Braintree, an old market (Wednesday
and Saturday) town which only just misses inclusion in this
chapter. The town's medieval prosperity was founded on the wool
industry, boosted by the arrival of Flemish weavers. The 18th
century demise of this industry was fortunately accompanied by
the start of the silk industry by Courtaulds.

The **Braintree District Museum** in Manor Street, open throughout
the year other than Mondays, tells the story of the town's diverse
local industrial heritage. There is also a natural history gallery. At
New Mills in South Street, the **Working Silk Museum** uses mid-
19th century hand looms, producing silk fabric from the raw
material. The museum is open daily other than weekends.

An excursion to Braintree could well be combined with a visit to
Kelvedon, where the Fearing and Kelvedon Local History Museum
contains Roman artefacts and agricultural bygones and also to
Cressing Temple, where two great medieval barns, built by monks of
the Knights Templar, have been renovated and provided with visitor
facilities, including refreshments.

Events: Colchester & North Essex

Maldon Carnival
Early August.

Wivenhoe Festival
Late May to late August,
sporadic entertainment
throughout the town.
☎ 01206 826699

Wivenhoe Carnival
Early June.
☎ 01206 306463

Clacton Air Show
Marine Parade. Late August.

Clacton Jazz Festival
Late August.

Walton Folk Festival
Walton on the Naze.
Mid-April.

Colchester History Fair
Castle Park. Mid-June.

Thaxted Music Festival
June and July.
☎ 01371 831421.

**Thaxted Fayre and
Gardeners' Weekend**
September.

Hotels

Colchester

Forte Posthouse
110 rooms, modern hotel
with pool and gymnasium
☎ 01206 767740 Fax 766577

The Butterfly Hotel
50 rooms, modern hotel
☎ 01206 230900 Fax 231095

The George Hotel
Old coaching inn in the
centre now luxuriously
equipped, 45 rooms
☎ 01206 578494 Fax 761732

Earls Colne

Riverside Motel
11 rooms, 16km (10 miles)
from Colchester
☎ and Fax 01787 223487

Dedham

Maison Talbooth
10 suites, deluxe small hotel
and renowned restaurant
☎ 01206 322367 Fax 322752

Harwich

The Pier
6 rooms, luxury hotel under
same ownership as above
☎ 01255 241212 Fax 551922

Clacton-on-Sea

Esplanade Hotel, 31 rooms
☎ 01255 220450 Fax 221800

Maldon

Neptune Cafe and Motel
Latchingdon, 10 rooms
☎ 01621 740770

Guest Houses and B&B

Nr Manningtree

**New House Farm
Country Guest House**
Wix, convenient for port
of Harwich
☎ 01255 870365 Fax 870837

Aldhams
Lawford, Queen Anne house
in 3 acres ☎ 01206 393210

Colchester

D'Arcy House
Culver Street East, town
centre guest house
☎ 01206 768111 Fax 763938

Self-catering

Colchester

Castle Road Cottages
☎ and Fax 01206 262210
Birds Farm, Elmstead Market
☎ 01206 823838

University of Essex
Large number of self-con-
tained flats available from
early July to late September
☎ 01206 872456 Fax 872464

Castle Hedingham
Rosemary Farm 2 cottages
☎ 01787 461653

Caravan and Camping Sites

Colchester

Colchester Camping
Conveniently situated site,
generally of a good standard

but some road noise
☎ and Fax 01206 545551

Mersea Island
Waldegraves Holiday Park
Many facilities including pool
and private slipway
☎ 01206 382898 Fax 385359

Eating Out

Colchester
Jacklin's Restaurant
147 High Street
☎ 01206 572157

Traders Bar and Grill
The Posthouse
☎ 01206 767740

Dedham
Maison Talbooth, up-market
restaurant, highly recom-
mended ☎ 01206 322367
Fax 322752

Harwich
The Pier, same ownership as
Maison Talbooth, emphasis
on fish in the restaurant
☎ 01255 241212
Fax 01255 551922

Thaxted
The Cake Table Tearoom,
award winning tea shop
☎ 01371 831206

Clacton-on-Sea
The Olive Branch Brasserie
at Thorpe le Soken
☎ 01255 861199

Nr East Bergholt
Tearoom at Bridge Cottage

Flatford Mill ☎ 01206 298260

Public Transport

Trains
Essex generally has above
average rail services, rural
north Essex less so than the
south of the county.

The main Norwich, Ipswich,
Colchester, Chelmsford &
London line has stations at
Manningtree, Colchester and
Marks Tey.

The Colchester to Walton
and Clacton branch line has
intermediate stations at
Wivenhoe, Alresford, Great
Bentley, Weeley, Thorpe le
Soken, Kirby Cross and
Frinton.

The branch which leaves the
main line at Manningtree
reaches Harwich via intermediate stations at Mistley,
Wrabness and Parkeston Quay.

Sudbury has its own branch
line, leaving the main line at
Marks Tey. The intermediate
stations are at Chappel, Wakes
Colne and Bures.

Buses
For information contact Essex
Bus, ☎ 0345 000333.

The Sunday Rover dis-
counted fare system has many
routes in north Essex which
are operational all year round,
Colchester being the focal
point. A summer-only route is
available across the more
remote area of Finchingfield
and Thaxted.

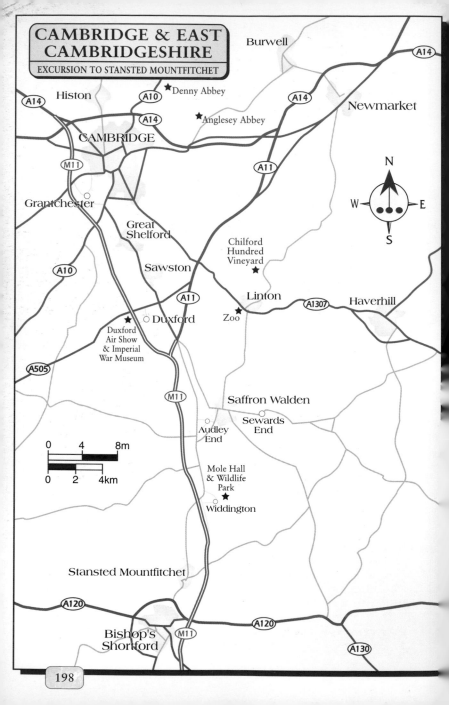

CAMBRIDGE & EAST CAMBRIDGESHIRE

9

This is a comparatively small area, dominated by a great city; not great in the sense of area or population, in both of which it is exceeded by many towns, but great in history, great in its array of wonderful old buildings and even greater in its world scale educational and academic influence. It is also a city of regional strategic significance, much sought after as a place to establish light industry and commerce and as a place to live, a cause of major planning problems.

North of Cambridge, the Fens (Chapter 1) reach close to the city. To the south of the city the countryside is gently rural and richly agricultural, rising and falling to the county boundary close to Saffron Walden. Saffron Walden, just inside Essex, together with Newmarket, which is just inside Suffolk, combines with villages, stately homes and other attractions to offer considerable visitor interest outside the city itself.

Above: The Backs, Cambridge

Saffron Walden
to Newmarket

At the south end of the area, the rural market town of **Saffron Walden** is an endearing place, rich in timber-framed and colour-washed buildings. Overhanging first floors confirm the great age of several and there are examples of elaborate pargetting, most notable being the Sun Inn on the corner of Market Hill and Church Street. The Market Place has a cross and a lovely timber framed Guildhall over a stone arcade. Another fine building is now used as a youth hostel. There are markets each Tuesday and Saturday.

Saffron

The name Saffron derives from a particular type of crocus (sativus), grown locally as a commercial crop from the 15th to 18th centuries. Highly prized and expensive, it was used as medicine, dye and flavouring.

Standing on a mound above the compact town centre is the great flint structure of **St Mary the Virgin,** biggest parish church in Essex.

The **Fry Gallery,** well situated in the Victorian landscaped Bridge End Gardens, just off Castle Street, specialises in the work of a group of artists based on nearby Great Bardfield, broadly from the 1920s to the present, with changing exhibitions. The work of founder L.G. Fry (1860-1933) is on permanent display. Best known of the group is Edward Bawden, who is well represented in the gallery.

Saffron Walden Museum, in Museum Street, is strong on social history, decorative arts, ethnography, archaeology, geology and natural history. There is also an Egyptian room. The scant ruins of a 12th century castle are situated in the museum grounds.

The town has good, close-knit, shopping and refreshment facilities. The nearest railway station is at Audley End, 3km (2 miles) away.

Audley End House and Gardens is one of the nation's great stately homes, built in 1605-14 by Thomas Howard, 1st Earl of Suffolk and remodelled during the 18th and 19th centuries, the rooms and furniture by Robert Adam. More than 30 rooms are open to the public; the furniture, silver and natural history collections are magnificent and there are paintings by Canaletto, Lely and Kneller. The park was landscaped by Lancelot 'Capability' Brown and has a miniature railway, operational at weekends and school holidays. Introductory talks about the house and its history are available.

A few kilometres to the north-west at **Duxford Airfield,** an outpost of the **Imperial War Museum** is a major attraction. Use the A505 to trespass across the M11, otherwise our western boundary for this part of East Anglia. Huge hangars by the side of the runway contain literally dozens of historic aircraft, whilst some large commercial planes, including a Concorde prototype, stand outside. Overall, this is the largest and best aircraft collection in Britain.

Because of the vast area covered by the museum, free transport by a little road train is provided. Towards the far end is a relatively new building, an award winning design housing the American Air Museum. Another feature is the Land Warfare Hall, which includes the Regimental exhibitions of the Royal Anglian Regiment and the Cambridgeshire Regiment. As would be expected, visitor facilities, including refreshments, are comprehensive.

Return across M11 and turn left before reaching the A1301 to find **Duxford Chapel**, close to Whittlesford station. The building is a rare survival, a former medieval hospital chapel. It is the only remaining portion of the 13th century Hospital of St John, built by the local Lord of the Manor. Monks, with lay assistance, sheltered poor travellers and tended to the sick. By the 14th century it had become a chantry, closed in 1547 by the Dissolution, following which it became a barn. It was restored about 400 years later. If closed, a key is available from the cottage across the road.

Linton Zoo is about 11km (7 miles) to the east, on the B1052 south of Linton village. The zoo is set in 4.8 hec (16 acres) of landscaped gardens, with a collection of animals which includes tigers and snow leopards. Conservation of species is a prime objective and the zoo participates in the inter-zoo breeding scheme. For children, quiz trails, pony rides, bouncy castle and play area all add to the attraction. In high season a cafeteria supplements the picnic area.

Three kilometres (2 miles) to the north, at **Chilford Halls**, an 7hec (18 acres) vineyard, one of the largest in East Anglia, is part of a larger estate. Several varieties of grape are grown and the wine making is by traditional methods. Personally guided tours and tasting are available for visitors, enhanced by a display of sculptures, a fine art print studio and the Vineleaf Cafe.

Head north-east to **Newmarket**, a single purpose town, the home of horse racing in Britain for many centuries, with more than 2,500 horses in training at any one time. The numerous training establishments are supplemented by the National Stud, the National Horse Racing Museum and the offices of the Jockey Club, the sport's ruling body.

Race meetings, using two courses on Newmarket Heath, are frequent. The first recorded race was in 1622, but the sport is older than that. King Charles II was a great and able enthusiast, winning the Town Plate on two occasions.

The town which supports this equine activity is pleasant but undistinguished; one long main street with the Jubilee clock tower at one end and a shopping area at the Market Square.

The **National Horse Racing Museum** is at 99, High Street. It displays the story of horse racing from its royal origins to modern times. A special feature is an 'equine tour', a comprehensive view behind the scenes of several yards and studs, led by expert guides. The tours begin at 09.20 on each day (other than Sunday) that the museum is open. Numbers are limited and advance booking is advised.

The **National Stud** is 3km (2 miles) south-west of the town, beside the July racecourse. Visitors (by appointment) are invited to meet stallions, mares and young foals and are offered a 75-minute guided tour. The visitor facilities include refreshments.

Cambridge

Cambridge was the site of a 1st century settlement constructed by a Belgic tribe on what is now Castle Hill. In AD40 the Romans took over this site, which then became a link along the road connecting the important Roman bases at Colchester and Lincoln.

Duxford Imperial War Museum

Fry Art Gallery

Off Castle Street, Saffron Walden. Open from Easter Sunday to the last Sunday in October and on Bank Holidays during this period, Saturday and Sunday, 14.45 to 17.30. ☎ 01799 513779.

Saffron Walden Museum

Museum Street. Open January, February, November, December, Monday to Saturday, 10.00 to 16.00; Sunday, 14.30 to 16.30. March to end of Oct, Monday to Saturday, 10.00 to 17.00; Sunday 14.30 to 17.00. Mid-April to the end of October, Bank Holiday Mondays, 14.30 to 17.00. Closed on 24th and 25th December.
☎ 01799 510333.

Audley End House and Gardens

English Heritage. Picnic area. Miniature railway (weekends and school holidays). Open from the beginning of April to the end of September, Wednesday to Sunday and Bank Holidays, 11.00 to 18.00. October, Wednesday to Sunday, 10.00 to 15.00.
☎ 01799 522399.

Imperial War Museum

Duxford Airfield. Open Jan to mid-May, daily, 10.00 to 16.00. Mid-May to late Oct, daily, 10.00 to 18.00. Late Octr to the end of Dec, daily, 10.00 to 16.00. Closed on 24th to 26th Dec.
☎ 01223 835000.

Linton Zoo

Cafeteria (high season only), picnic area. Children's activities. Open daily all year except Christmas Day, 10.00 to 18.00, or dusk if earlier.
☎ 01223 891308.

Chilford Halls Vineyard

Open from Good Friday to the end of October, 11.00 to 17.30. ☎ 01223 892641.

National Horseracing Museum

Newmarket. Cafe and gift shop. Open from early March to the end of October, daily, 10.00 to 17.00. Closed each Monday, except Bank Holidays and Mondays during July and August.
☎ 01638 667333.

The National Stud

Newmarket. Open from early March to the end of August, daily, by appointment.
☎ 01638 663464.

Later the Saxons occupied the site, followed by the Normans who built their castle on the same mound, largely as a base for subjugating Saxon rebels, in particular Hereward the Wake and his followers.

Growth through medieval times is largely the story of the development of the University, college ·by college over the centuries, to produce one of the world's greatest centres of learning, a bonding of more than 30 individual colleges supported by a great array of ancillary academic institutes. The first scholars arrived in Cambridge in 1209, reputedly having left Oxford in dispute with the authorities, and the first college, **Peterhouse**, was founded by the Bishop of Ely in 1284.

The following three centuries saw the foundation of 15 further colleges. The majority of these colleges are centrally located; their foundation by Kings, Queens, Bishops and Nobles, and powerful patronage, has ensured that the endowments were lavish, the resultant wealth producing great architectural treasures concentrated in the heart of the city. Sir Christopher Wren was just one of the great architects involved. The newer colleges are, of necessity, further from the city centre, but all can be reached on foot without difficulty.

Space does not permit individual description of each college; most visitors stroll around in a general way, absorbing the atmosphere and perhaps focusing on just a few of the highlights. Most of the colleges allow public admission to a greater or lesser extent; all have their own rules, some are free, some make a charge.

The Backs of several colleges are known throughout the world as being linked by a pedestrian route on the far side of the River Cam, with cows grazing just a short distance from the bustle of the city centre. The river wends its way serenely through the city, disturbed only by water fowl and the gentle swish of the punts, traditional flat-bottomed boats with an unusual form of propulsion. The river bridges are worth a close look, those associated with the 'Backs' walk being Mathematical, Kings, Clare, Garret Hostel, Trinity, Kitchen and Bridge of Sighs.

Other Attractions

Of the numerous university buildings, many of them famous in their own right, which underpin the work of the colleges, pride of place goes to the **Fitzwilliam Museum**, an elegant building on Trumpington Street, built in 1834. The collection of paintings, antiquities, ceramics and much more is outstanding, altogether worthy of its role in this learned city.

The **Cambridge and County Folk Museum**, at 2/3, Castle

Street has nine display rooms housed in a late 15th century timber-framed building. The theme is the everyday life of the people of Cambridge and the surrounding area from 1600 to the present day.

Kettle's Yard, also in Castle Street, has a collection of 20th century art in a unique domestic setting and a comprehensive programme of recitals, chamber music, exhibitions and workshops.

In concentrating on the colleges, the **city's churches** should not be overlooked; the university church is St Mary's in Trinity Street, noted for the views from its 17th century tower. The Holy Sepulchre, close to Bridge Street, is one of only four round churches in Britain, now being used as a brass rubbing centre. St Benet's, beside Corpus Christi, is the oldest church in Cambridgeshire, with an Anglo-Saxon tower.

Throughout the year there are daily guided tours of the city, more frequent during the season, conducted by expert guides, operating from the **Tourist Information Centre**. During the summer, cruises in Aquarius, an all-weather 60 seater river cruiser start at Jesus Green.

In such an overwhelmingly academic environment it would be easy to forget that Cambridge is also very much a working city of regional significance, with the shopping centre, offices and supporting buildings such as theatres and cinemas largely crammed in a central area among the colleges. The **'Park and Ride'** system, operated by Stagecoach Cambus from four points outside the city is recommended.

The shops include a high proportion of individual traders, book shops being particularly well represented. A general market is held on Market Hill from Monday to Saturday. With a huge student population the range of entertainment is much as would be expected, with music from folk to pop to classical and a good variety of theatre. Many of the venues are in college buildings.

The railway station has fast services to and from London, both Kings Cross and Liverpool Street. More local services include the line across Suffolk to Ipswich; Ely (for Norwich), and Peterborough, where connections to the Midlands and the Northeast are available. Some of the London trains continue along the branch to Kings Lynn.

By the side of the A1303, about 5km (3 miles) from the city centre, the beautifully landscaped **American Military Cemetery** is a fitting memorial to nearly 4000 American servicemen killed in World War II who are buried here, and to more than 5000 who have no known grave but whose names are inscribed on the memorial wall. This is claimed to be the only World War II cemetery in the British Isles.

Fitzwilliam Museum

Trumpington Street. Cafe and gift shop. Open daily, Tuesday to Saturday, 10.00 to 17.00; Sunday, 14.15 to 17.00. Also open on August Bank Holiday Monday. Closed over Xmas. ☎ 01223 332900.

Cambridge and County Folk Museum

Castle Street. Open from April to September, Monday to Saturday, 10.30 to 17.00; Sunday, 14.00 to 17.00. October to March, Tuesday to Saturday, 10.30 to 17.00; Sunday, 14.00 to 17.00. ☎ 01223 355159.

Kettle's Yard

Castle Street. House open Tuesday to Sunday, 14.00 to 16.00. Gallery open Tuesday to Saturday, 12.30 to 17.30; Sunday, 14.00 to 17.30. Closed over Xmas. ☎ 01223 352124.

Cambridge River Cruises

Operational daily during Easter Week and from April to September. More frequent sailings in June July and August. ☎ 01223 300 100.

American Military Cemetery

Coton, Cambridge. Open daily from the beginning of January to mid-April and from the beginning of October to the end of December, 08.00 to 17.00. Mid-April to the end of September, daily, 08.00 to 18.00. ☎ 01954 210350.

The ancient colleges fall geographically into two main groups. Those along the main thoroughfare, Trumpington Street, King's Parade, Trinity Street, St John's Street are, from the south, Peterhouse, Pembroke, Corpus Christi, St Catherine's, Queen's, King's, Clare, Trinity Hall, Gonville and Caius, Trinity and St John's. Across the river, Magdalen stands a little apart.

The second group, strung along another long street, with the names Regent Street, St Andrew's Street, Sidney Street, comprises Downing, Emmanuel, Christ's and Sidney Sussex. Standing more isolated to the north-east is Jesus. Some features of particular note are the beautiful Tudor gatehouse at St John's, an array of lovely buildings at Trinity and Sir Christopher Wren's first complete design (1666) at Pembroke.

Although there are interesting features, such as sculpture by Henry Moore and Barbara Hepworth at Churchill and a fine little chapel with stained glass at Robinson, on the whole the architecture of the modern colleges is uninspiring.

King's College

Perhaps paramount in the awesome architectural collection of Cambridge is King's College, with royal associations from King Henry VI onwards. The chapel is magnificent; the long, narrow nave makes an immediate impact with high walls and great windows soaring to the wonderful fan-vaulted roof.

The dark oak screen has the initials of King Henry VIII and Anne Boleyn, whilst Rubens' *Adoration of the Magi*, behind the altar, provides decoration of the highest order; an exhibition records the creation of the chapel. The annual televised service of nine lesson and carols each Christmas brings the chapel and its celebrated choir into millions of homes worldwide.

Far left: The South doorway to King's College Chapel
Left: St John's College Gateway, Cambridge

Grantchester

How better to finish this chapter and, indeed, the whole book than by taking a leisurely tea at **Grantchester**, a traditional activity for generations of Cambridge students, tutors and other academics? Not much more than a mile separates this quiet village from the hustle and bustle of Cambridge and there is a delightful easy footpath by the side of the River Cam. The Orchard tearoom has hosted Maynard Keynes, Bertrand Russell, Augustus John, Ludwig Wittgenstein, E.M. Forster, Virginia Woolf, Rupert Brooke and countless others, famous and less so, in its spacious orchard since 1897. Grantchester was Brooke's home village, first as a lodger at Orchard House and later at the Old Vicarage, next door. On a trip to Berlin, homesickness for the idyllic life in Grantchester inspired one of his best loved poems - *The Old Vicarage*; the closing lines of which:

*'Stands the church clock at
ten to three
And is there honey still for tea'*

have endured as a marvellously concise evocation of timelessness in this quintessentially English village and tea garden.

Sadly, Brooke died at the age of 27, on a troopship en route for Gallipoli. A short time earlier, as part of his poem, *The Soldier* he had written his other most widely known lines:

*'If I should die, think only
this of me:
That there's some corner of
a foreign field
That is forever England'.*

Touching such a deep chord, his posthumous place in the national consciousness was assured.

Apart from The Orchard, Grantchester has pretty buildings and an inn along the roadside. A short footpath along one side of The Old Vicarage leads to a willow-lined pond and an old mill.

 Walks: Cambridgeshire

The footpath mentioned above under 'Grantchester' has prime place as a short, easy, stroll.

Designated paths passing through this area include part of the **Icknield Way**, a route which largely follows ancient tracks from Ivinghoe Beacon in the south-west of the country to join the **Peddars Way** (see Chapter 2) near Thetford. It can be reached at Great Chesterford and Linton; there is also a Roman road from

Cambridge to the south-east which runs to join the Icknield Way at a point north-east of Linton in about 25km (15 miles). It is open to walkers, cyclists and horse riders.

The attractive countryside around **Saffron Walden** is well covered 'Walden Walks' in a series of local leaflets. The circuits are all at the gentle end of the scale, ranging from about 3km to 7km (2 to 4.25 miles) in length. A good example is a walk at Sewards End, a little way to the east of Saffron Walden.

Sewards End Walk

From the village hall car park walk along the roadside. Opposite the water tower cross the road and take the footpath past the tower. Soon there is a double signpost. A right turn here gives a walk of approx. 3km (2 miles). For the main route, about 5.5km (3.5 miles), turn left, with a hedge to the right.

At a farm track cross diagonally left to take a gravel track around Hoys Farm Cottage. Go straight on, cross a ditch on the right and continue with a hedge on the left. At a road turn right and then, in 150m (164 yards), turn right again, over a stile. Go across a field to a junction of trees and wire fence. Cross a stile and pass a pond surrounded by trees. There is another stile to cross before Reedings Grove is reached. Follow the path to the left through the wood, then right, with trees on the right.

Go straight on, passing Hoys Farm and then Frogs Green Farm (just before Frogs Green Farm the short route joins from the right). Turn right over a stile, crossing an open field to another stile in the hedge. Bear slightly right to cross another open field to the corner of trees and continue ahead with trees on the left. Follow the path through a gap with the trees now on the right.

Go through another gap and across an open field towards a line of big trees which screen 'The Towers'. Turn right over two plank bridges. After passing a wire fence on the right and then Tower Lodge on the left, the road is reached. Turn right to return to the car park.

↑1 **Montfichet Castle**, near Stanstead, where the only reconstructed Norman motte and bailey castle in the world is well
worth a visit and has a considerable programme of events. A **Toy
Museum** is near by. The excursion can readily be combined with the
Mole Hall Wildlife Park and Butterfly Pavilion at Widdington, where
a good range of animals is backed by comprehensive visitor
facilities. Otter feeding time is particularly popular.

↑2 **St Neots and Huntingdon** This tour heads west from
Cambridge, to a pair of attractive country market towns,
both with historical associations backed by museums. Oliver
Cromwell was born at Huntingdon. Both towns also have river
boating facilities on the Great Ouse. Market days are Thursday
(St Neots) and Wednesday and Saturday (Huntingdon).

↑3 **The Dick Turpin Heritage Route** About 80km (50 miles) in
length. Saffron Walden is a good starting and finishing place
for this circuit, which visits small towns such as Thaxted, and
several villages including Finchingfield and Turpin's birthplace at
Hempstead. A leaflet setting out the whole route is obtainable
from Tourist Information Centres in the area.

Events: Cambridge & East Cambridgeshire

**Cambridge
Annual Film Festival**
Cambridge Arts Cinema.
Mid-to late July.

Cambridge Folk Festival
Cherry Hinton Hall.
Late July to early August.

'Bumps' Races
Rowing eights on the River
Cam. June and July.

Summer in the City
A programme of music and
other events in Cambridge
during the summer.

Midsummer Fair
Midsummer Common. June.

Summer Recitals
An extensive programme
of music. Mid-July to
mid-August.

**Duxford Air Show
Imperial War Museum,
Duxford**
Early September.

Keeping away from main roads, the south-eastern part of Cambridgeshire is ideal cycling country, never uncomfortably hilly but sufficiently rolling to produce attractive countryside. A circular ride of about 46km (30 miles) to the south from Saffron Walden to Montfichet Castle and/or the Wildlife Park and Butterfly Pavilion at Widdington would make a fine outing.

Like many university centres, Cambridge is a bicycle city, with students and others resorting to this cheap and efficient means of transport. In addition to standard cycle hire, **Geoff's Bike Hire** at 65, Devonshire Road, close to the railway station, also offers 2-hour guided cycle tours around the Cambridge colleges each Tuesday, Wednesday, Thursday and Saturday, from April to September. Guided tours along quiet lanes to surrounding villages are also available. ☎ 01223 365629.

Additional Information

Hotels

Cambridge

University Arms
City centre 115 rooms
☎ 01223 351241

Arundel House Hotel
Chesterton Road, within walking distance of city centre, 100 rooms ☎ 01223 367701 Fax 01223 367721

Moat House Hotel, about 10km (6 miles) from the city, 99 rooms ☎ 01954 249988 Fax 780010

Holiday Inn
Downing Street, 196 rooms
☎ 01223 464466 Fax 464440

Panos Hotel
10 minutes walk to railway station, 7 rooms
☎ 01223 212958

Duxford

Duxford Lodge, set in an acre of garden and convenient for both Newmarket and Cambridge Small, luxurious, hotel with 15 rooms
☎ 01223 836444 Fax 832271

Saffron Waldon

The Crown House
☎ 01799 530515 Fax 530683

Newmarket

Bedford Lodge Hotel and Conference Centre
☎ 01638 663175

Rutland Arms Hotel
☎ 01638 664251

Heath Court Hotel
☎ 01638 667171

Guest Houses and B&B

Cambridge

The Suffolk House
Milton Road
☎ 01223 352016 Fax 566816

Moat House Farm
Comberton, 5 miles from
Cambridge ☎ 01223 263978

Swaffham Bulbeck

The Old Rectory
☎ and Fax 01223 811986

Nr Saffron Waldon

Rockells Farm
Duddenhoe End
☎ 01763 838053 Fax 837001

Self-catering

Cambridge

Clarence House
13 Clarendon Street, 4
apartments
☎ and Fax 01223 841294

Saffron Walden

Whitensmere Farm Cottages
Ashdon, 3 properties
☎ 01799 584244

Waterbeach

Goose Hall Farm Cottages
☎ 01223 860235

Caravan and Camping Sites

Cambridge

Cherry Hinton Caravan Club Site, very convenient for city
☎ 01223 244088

Highfield Farm Camping Park
Comberton 6km (4 miles)
from city ☎ 01223 262308

Stanford Park Caravan Site
Burwell 13km (8 miles) from
city ☎ 01638 741547

Eating Out

Cambridge

Midsummer House,
award winning restaurant
☎ 01223 369299

Hobbs Pavilion Restaurant
☎ 01223 674480

Browns Restaurant
23, Trumpington Street
☎ 01223 461655

The Three Horseshoes
at Madingley 3km (2 miles)
from Cambridge, restaurant
and snacks at the bar
☎ 01954 210221

Grantchester

The Orchard Tea Gardens
a unique experience

Nr Newmarket

The Star Inn
Lidgate
☎ 01638 500275

Tuddenham Mill Restaurant
Tuddenham St Mary
☎ 01638 713552

Public Transport

Trains

Services available from Cambridge are set out in the main text.
Other stations in this area are Newmarket-Cambridge to
Ipswich line; Great Shelford, Whittlesford, Great Chesterford
and Audley End-Cambridge to London (Liverpool Street) line.

Buses

In the city area of Cambridge bus services are comprehensive
including the centre and the various suburbs. The Park and
Ride system has already been mentioned; The Grafton Centre is
the focal point of this four route system (service nos. 500, 501,
502, 503) and the outlying car parks are at Madingley Road,
Cowley Road, Clifton Road and Newmarket Road.

For leisure travel the Sunday Rover discounted ticket- 'buy
one ticket, travel all day, save pounds' is again recommended
for this area. Services go in many directions from Cambridge,
Saffron Walden and Newmarket. Visitor attractions such as
Audley End offer a discounted admission charge to the holders
of a ticket.

LANDMARK
Publishing Ltd ● ● ● ●

Other Landmark Visitors Guides to Britain
'Pack 2 months into 2 weeks'

Cornwall & the Isles of Scilly
ISBN:
1 901522 09 1
256pp, Full colour,
£9.99

West Cornwall
ISBN:
1 901522 24 5
96pp, Full colour,
£4.95

Devon
ISBN:
1 901522 42 3
224pp, Full colour,
£9.95

South Devon
ISBN:
1 901522 52 0
96pp, Full colour,
£4.95

Peak District
ISBN:
1 901522 25 3
240pp, Full colour,
£9.99

Southern Peak
District
ISBN:
1 901522 27 X
96pp, Full colour,
£4.95

Lake District
ISBN:
1 901522 38 5
224pp, Full colour,
£9.95

Southern
Lakeland
ISBN:
1 901522 53 9
96pp, Full colour,
£4.95

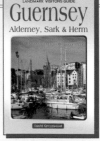
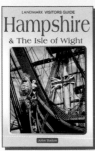

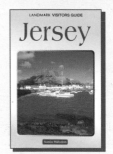

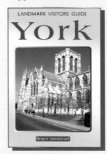

Fact File

ACCOMMODATION

There is accommodation available to suit all needs and budgets throughout East Anglia: luxury hotels, secluded country hotels, lodges for travellers, hospitable pubs, bed and breakfast in private houses, farm accommodation, self-catering cottages and apartments from basic to de-luxe, youth hostels and bunk houses.

Particularly in the larger hotels, there can be huge variations in tariff, with many special offers available for out of season breaks, mid-week or weekend bargain offers; it is well worth shopping around If calling personally at any establishment before making a reservation, it is quite acceptable to ask to see the available room.

Whilst some of the establishments listed are known to the authors, the inclusion in this book does not necessarily constitute a recommendation.

The listings below provide a sample of accommodation and restaurants available; more extensive lists may be obtained from the relevant Tourist Information Centre where, in the majority of cases, a reservation service is provided.

SELF-CATERING: COTTAGES, APARTMENTS AND CARAVANS

There are agents who offer a choice of property to rent, usually on a weekly basis but sometimes for shorter periods The size of the property, its facilities, and the rent vary considerably; most are considerably cheaper out of the main holiday season

It is also possible to rent properties directly from the owner; these are advertised in weekend newspapers and in magazines such as **The Lady**; many are listed in booklets obtainable from Tourist Information Centres.

Some agencies offering self-catering accommodation:

North Norfolk Holiday Homes
130 properties throughout the area ☎ 01328 855322

Norfolk Country Cousins
90 properties Freephone 0500400407

Norfolk Country Cottages
Good selection of properties available ☎ 01603 871872

Suffolk and Norfolk Country Cottages
Many properties available ☎ and Fax 271350

BOAT HIRE

Most of the major and some minor boating centres have boatyards from which motor cruisers and day boats can be hired.

A smaller number also have sailing boats See also Chapter 1 feature 'Boating in the Fens' and Chapter 4, 'Pleasure Boating on the Broads'.

Blakes Holidays Ltd
Wroxham ☎ 01603 784458

Broads Tours Ltd
Wroxham ☎ 01603 782207

Broom Boats Ltd Riverside
Brundall ☎ 01603 714803

Highcraft
Thorpe St Andrew, Norwich
☎ 01603 701701

Scudamores Boatyards
Mill Lane, Granta Place,
Cambridge ☎ 01223 359750

**Norfolk Broads
Yachting Co Ltd**
Lower Street, Horning
☎ 01692 631330

River Craft
The Staithe, Stalham
☎ 01692 580288

H.Woods
Broads Haven, Potter Heigham
☎ 01692 670711

Maestranl
Mill Lane Dedham
☎ 01206 323153

East Coaster Sailing
5, Prince Albert Road, Mersea Island
☎ 01206 382545

Secret Charters, 'Pippins'
Abberton Road, Layer-de-la-Haye, Colchester
☎ 01206 734727

Excursion boats operate from Wroxham, Horning, Norwich, Stalham and Oulton Broad.

GUIDES

The Registered Blue Badge Guide Scheme applies throughout East Anglia. All guides have attended an approved training scheme and can be identified when wearing the 'Blue Badge'. Lists of guides and details of tours are obtainable from:

East of England Tourist Board
Toppesfield Hall, Hadleigh, Suffolk, IP7 5DN
☎ 01473 822922

Note for group tours with a guide, advance notice, usually at least one week, is required.

HORSE RACING

Great Yarmouth Racecourse ☎ 01493 720343
Newmarket – England's premier racing centre, with important meetings on two racecourses.

MAPS

For the general visitor who likes to use a good map, there is nothing to beat the Ordnance Survey 'Landranger' (red) series. The scale of these maps is 1:50,000; the following sheets cover the area included in this book:

No 132   North West Norfolk
No 133   North East Norfolk
No 134   Norwich and the Broads Great Yarmouth
No 143   Ely and Wisbech Downham Market
No 144   Thetford and Diss, Breckland and Wymondham
No 154   Cambridge and Newmarket Saffron Walden
No 155   Bury St Edmunds Sudbury and Stowmarket
No 156   Saxmundham and Aldeburgh
No 168   Colchester Halstead and Maldon
No 169   Ipswich and the Naze Clacton on Sea

For more specialised requirements, the larger scale of 1:25,000 may be advantageous in its greater detail.

Outdoor Leisure (yellow) map no 40 (double sided) gives complete cover of the Norfolk and Suffolk Broads. The North Norfolk Coast is covered by three of the newer 'Explorer' (orange) maps, Nos 23, 24, 25, at the same large scale. The 'Explorer' maps are rapidly replacing the older small 'Pathfinders' (green) in areas not covered by 'Outdoor Leisure' maps.

NATURALISTS' ORGANISATIONS

Broads Authority
18, Colegate, Norwich
☎ 01603 610734

**The National
Trust Blickling**
Norwich
☎ 01263 733471

Norfolk Wildlife Trust
72, Cathedral Close, Norwich
☎ 01603 625540

**Royal Society for the
Protection of Birds**
65, Thorpe Road, Norwich
☎ 01603 661662

English Nature
60, Brancondale, Norwich
☎ 01603 620558

Norfolk Ornithologists' Association
Aslack Way, Holme next the Sea, Hunstanton
☎ 01485 525406

Suffolk Wildlife Trust
Brooke House, The Green, Ashbocking, Ipswich
☎ 01473 890089

Essex Wildlife Trust
Fingringhoe Wick Nature Reserve, Colchester
☎ 01206 729678

The Wildlife Trust for Cambridgeshire
Enterprise House, Maris Lane, Trumpington, Cambridge
☎ 01223 846363

SPECIALIST HOLIDAYS AND ACTIVITIES

Byways Bicycles, Darsham
Saxmundham, Suffolk Cycling holidays
☎ 01728 668764

Weekend packages
foot, punt and bicycle
☎ 01223 502134

Hilltop Adventure
Oldwood, Beeston Regis, Sheringham Outdoor activities
☎ 01263 824514

Grand Touring Club
Model Farm, Rattlesden, Bury St Edmunds. Short hotel breaks with use of vintage sports car, balloon flights and other specialised activities
☎ 01449 373774

Norfolk Church Tours
Half-day tours of four country churches
☎ 01603 811542

Snape Maltings
Painting, crafts and decorative arts courses
☎ 01728 688305

Suffolk Cycle Breaks
Cycling and walking holidays throughout Suffolk ☎ 01449 721555

Thornham Field Centre,
Near Eye, Suffolk Includes craft workshop
☎ 01379 788153

TOURIST INFORMATION CENTRES

* indicates not open all year
NORFOLK

Aylsham
Bure Valley Station,
☎ 01263 733903

Cromer
Bus Station,
☎ 01263 512497

Fact File

Diss
Meres Mouth, Mere Street
☎ 01379 650523

***Fakenham**
Market Place
☎ 01328 851981

***Great Yarmouth**
Marine Parade
☎ 01493 842195

***Hoveton**
Station Road
☎ 01603 782281

Hunstanton
Town Hall, The Green
☎ 01485 532610

Kings Lynn
☎ 01553 763044

***Mundesley**
2a, Station Road
☎ 01263 721070

Norwich
The Guildhall, Gaol Hill
☎ 01603 666071

***Sheringham**
Station Approach
☎ 01263 824329

***Walsingham**
Common Place
☎ 01328 820510

***Wells-next-the-Sea**
Staithe Street
☎ 01328 710885

SUFFOLK

***Aldeburgh**
The Cinema, High Street
☎ 01728 453637

***Beccles**
The Quay, Fen Lane
☎ 01502 713196

Bury St Edmunds
6, Angel Hill
☎ 01284 764667

Felixstowe
Leisure Centre,
☎ 01394 276770

Hadleigh
Toppesfield Hall
☎ 01473 823824

Ipswich
St Stephens Lane
☎ 01473 258070

***Lavenham**
Lady Street
☎ 01787 248207

Lowestoft
East Point Pavilion,
☎ 01502 523000

Newmarket
63, The Rookery
☎ 01638 667200

***Southwold**
Town Hall, Market Place
☎ 01502 724729

Stowmarket
Wilkes Way
☎ 01449 676800

Sudbury
Town Hall, Market Hill
☎ 01787 881320

Woodbridge, Station Buildings
☎ 01394 382240

ESSEX

Clacton on Sea
3, Pier Avenue
☎ 01255 423400

Colchester
1, Queen Street
☎ 01206 282920

Harwich
Parkeston ☎ 01255 506139

Maldon
Coach Lane
☎ 01621 856503

Saffron Walden
1, Market Place,
☎ 01799 510444

CAMBRIDGESHIRE

Cambridge
Wheeler Street
☎ 01223 322640

Ely
29, St Mary's Street
☎ 01353 662062

Wisbech
2-3 Bridge Street, Ely Place
☎ 01945 583263

TRANSPORT

RAIL AND BUS

Rail information for the whole of East Anglia,
24 hours, 7 days a week ☎ 0345 484950

Norfolk Bus	☎ 0500 626116
Suffolk Bus	☎ 01473 583358
Essex Bus	☎ 0345 000333
Cambridgeshire Bus	☎ 01223 717740

FERRY SERVICES

Scandinavian Seaways, Harwich	☎ 0990 333 000
Stena Line, Harwich	☎ 01255 243333

AIRPORTS

Norwich Airport	☎ 01603 411923
Stansted Airport Bishop's Stortford	☎ 01279 680500
Cambridge Airport Teversham	☎ 01223 293621

CAR HIRE

Enterprise Rent a Car
☎ 01992 509990

Willhire Ltd
☎ 0345 161718

Kenning Car and Van Rental,
Several locations across
East Anglia
☎ 0541 55590

C & C Car and Van Hire, 67,
Layer Road, Colchester
☎ 01206 761011

• Index •

Published By
Landmark Publishing Ltd
Waterloo House, 12 Compton, Ashbourne,
Derbyshire DE6 1DA England
Tel: 01335 347349 e-mail: landmark@clara.net

1st Edition
ISBN 901522 58 X

British Library Cataloguing in Publication Data: a catalogue record
for this book is available from the British Library.

Print: UIC Printing & Packaging Pte Ltd, Singapore
Cartography: James Allsopp
Designed by: James Allsopp

Cover Pictures
Front: Ely Cathedral
Back T: Blicking Hall near Aylsham
Back B: Cavendish Village

Picture Credits:
Glyn Wingfield: Page 182
Keith Allsopp: Page 206
All other pictures are supplied by the authors